Donated to
Yreka Library by
Lolly Hammond Estate

You're Old, I'm Old . . .
Get Used to It!

**Center Point
Large Print**

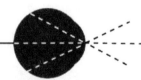

**This Large Print Book carries the
Seal of Approval of N.A.V.H.**

You're Old, I'm Old . . . Get Used to It!

20 Reasons Why Growing Old Is Great

Virginia Ironside

CENTER POINT LARGE PRINT
THORNDIKE, MAINE

This Center Point Large Print edition is
published in the year 2010 by arrangement with
Viking, a member of Penguin Group (USA) Inc.

The text of this Large Print edition is unabridged.
In other aspects, this book may vary
from the original edition.
Printed in the United States of America.
Set in 16-point Times New Roman type.

ISBN: 978-1-60285-914-2

Library of Congress Cataloging-in-Publication Data

Ironside, Virginia.
  You're old, i'm old— get used to it! / Virginia Ironside.
    p. cm.
  ISBN 978-1-60285-914-2 (library binding : alk. paper)
  1. Older people—Humor. 2. Old age—Humor. 3. Aging—Humor.
    4. Large type books. I. Title.
  HQ1061.I756 2010b
  305.26—dc22

                                                    2010024057

For Jennie

Contents

Introduction

No wise man ever wished to be younger.
—Swift

. . . . .

Between thirty and forty, one is distracted by
the Five Lusts;
Between seventy and eighty, one is a prey to
a hundred diseases.
But from fifty to sixty one is free from all ills;
Calm and still—the heart enjoys rest.
I have put behind me Love and Greed; I have
done with Profit and Fame.
I am still short of illness and decay and far
from decrepit age.
Strength of limb I still possess to seek the
rivers and hills;
Still my heart has spirit enough to listen to
flutes and strings.
At leisure I open new wine and taste several cups;
Drunken I recall old poems and sing a
whole volume.
—Po Chü (772–846)

. . . . .

9

Tomorrow I will haul down the flag of hypocrisy,
I will devote my grey hairs to wine:
My life's span has reached seventy.
If I don't enjoy life now, when shall I?
    —*The Rubáiyát of Omar Khayyam*

UNTIL VERY RECENTLY I'd never thought of old age as anything but frightful, something to be avoided at all costs. The prospect of being in one's sixties was hideous, particularly after the Beatles, in their rather condescending song, "When I'm Sixty-four," seemed to suggest that no one of that age did anything but mend fuses, knit sweaters, and dig up weeds in the garden.

To be honest, I've never liked being in the higher age range of any kind—even of each decade. So although I didn't mind finding I was thirty-one or forty-one, becoming thirty-nine or forty-nine was a different matter. From a young thirty- or forty-year-old, I turned into an old thirty- or forty-year-old. But once I was fifty-nine I wasn't too certain that the same magic as had been wreaked once I became a novice in other decades would continue to exert its power once I reached sixty. Like Doris Day, I thought that "the really frightening thing about middle age is the knowledge that you'll grow out of it."

And a friend of mine, upon reaching eighty, didn't help. "Those two fat circles on top of each other," he said, "followed by another great big circle. It's *grotesque*."

However, sixty isn't eighty, by any means. And I couldn't help getting a bit irritated when, hearing that I was about to reach the big six-oh, my friends started to get maddeningly sympathetic. "Oh, poor you," they said. Then they'd add, in a flattering whisper, "But you don't *look* it!" Then, a few moments later, "Don't worry, we won't say anything. And for heaven's sake, don't give a party—you don't want to advertise your age to the world!"

Indeed, lots of my friends tried to put some kind of youthful gloss on the whole aging process. "Sixty going on twenty!" they said, archly. But I couldn't help feeling that was nonsense. Sixty isn't "going on" twenty. It's not "going on" thirty either. The only place it's "going on" is seventy and then, if you're lucky (or unlucky, depending on your view) eighty.

Others said, "Sixty is really just fifty-ten!" The tweeness of it! Or, "Sixty is the new forty." But quite honestly I didn't know what they were talking about. You wouldn't say "Sea is the new land" or "Life is the new death" (or vice versa). Come off it.

Then there were those twinkling oldies who said, "You're only as old as you feel!" But you're *not* only as old as you feel. I may sound rather pedantic and Asperger's syndromish, but sixty is

11

sixty and thirty is thirty. The only people who think that sixty is young, in my experience, are seventy-year-olds, eighty-year-olds, and ninety-year-olds—in other words, the extremely old and the ancient.

Anyway, when I was twenty years old, sixty was terribly old. And when I was thirty, I felt that, at sixty, you had one foot in the grave. At forty, I was totally uninterested in old people—and that included sixty-year-olds. When I was fifty I started worrying a bit—oh Lord, "old" was getting pretty near. So now that I'm in my sixties myself (well, to be brutally frank, I'm sixty-five) I can't suddenly turn around and say, "Oh, whoops! I got it completely wrong! All those years I've been saying sixty is old and actually it's *not*. It's frightfully *young,* really. For the last fifty years I've been *totally deluded.*" It would be unfair to my younger self.

I started to wonder: Was this denial of age actually an old-fashioned view of aging? I always remember an old agony aunt (an advice columnist) friend of mine, now dead, who advised me never to tell anyone my age. "I always keep my age quiet," she confided. "It's nobody's business but mine."

But I've never been one for pretense. And what I couldn't bear was for anyone, when I'd been keeping quiet about my age, suddenly to find out how old I was behind my back. "You know,

Virginia . . . she's really sixty-five!" they'd say in a stage whisper. "No wonder she won't tell anyone how old she is!"

And I was amazed at how many of my contemporaries were still reluctant to admit they were old. Bonnie Greer, writing about her contemporaries born between 1944 and 1954, asserted in the *Independent*, "We just hang on and on, demanding our space, wanting our way, shielding our eyes from the writing on the wall. Our anthem was The Who line: 'Hope I die before I get old.' Trouble is we did not die *and* we refuse to grow old. So here we are, caught in the feeble embers of a long dead flame whose glow still manages to white out all those behind us."

It seems as if age is one of the last taboos. And so few people who *are* old want to talk about it. I often say things like, "I've only got a few years left so I might as well . . ." and everyone jumps up and down (insofar as any old person is capable of jumping up and down) and says, "Oh, don't say *that!*" as if by mentioning a limit to my future I'm actually courting death. I often refer to myself as "old" and contemporaries shout me down: "You're not old!" But what they mean is, "Don't say that! Because if *you're* old, *we're* old, and we desperately want not to be old! So don't let the team down!"

A friend of mine once said she was old to another friend, who immediately stopped her in her tracks. "Don't use that word!" she said, sharply. "You're not old—you're *mature!*"

"Mature?" replied my friend. "Certainly not! It sounds dangerously close to 'fermented'!"

I once wrote an article for AARP, the American Association of Retired People. It is a magazine *designed* for the elderly, and it has a readership of more than fifty million people. Well, I wrote the piece and sent it over to New York and then I got a proof back and was astonished to discover that during the whole piece, in which I had, naturally, used the word *old* quite a few times, those three letters together had been completely eradicated. So I rang up and left a message with the copy editor saying, "This is all very nice and the layout is fine, the photograph is lovely, the illustration is just dandy—but why have you removed the word *old* from the copy?"

I got back a call from a very quavery-voiced American woman who sounded about a hundred. "Oh, hi, Ginnie," she croaked. "I'm sorry that you're confused about the copyediting. But at AARP we don't like to use the word *old!*"

The American Association of Retired People not wanting to use the word *old?* It seems madness. Like trying to be a hairdresser without mentioning the word *shampoo.* Or talking about Monty Python without using the word *parrot.* To talk about age without using the word *old* sounds like one of those crazy parlor games where the trick is to talk for a minute without using the words *the* or *and*.

As my sixtieth birthday drew closer I found that I, too, was starting to get brainwashed into thinking that *old* was something ghastly, something to be avoided at all costs. It was only when the day actually came that I started to realize that being old isn't something to deny or hush up or apologize for.

Far from it.

It's something to *celebrate*.

It's true—sixty isn't the winter of anything. It's the springtime of old age. A poet once said, "The trouble with old age is that it is not interesting until one gets there. It's a foreign country, with an unknown language to the young and even to the middle-aged." And she was right. It *is* interesting. And liberating. And one of the many reasons it's fun is exactly contrary to so many of the myths that are currently promulgated.

Take that ludicrous line, "It's never too late!"

And yet that's one of the great things about being sixty. It *is* too late. It may sound daft, but for years I've been secretly imagining that one day, if I put my mind to it, I could still become a world-famous ballerina. Or a concert pianist. Or a record-breaking long-jumper. But finally—rather late, I grant you—I realized that these careers would be most unlikely. I look back and I see that all my life I have actually been a journalist. I also see that I have written and published fifteen books. It doesn't take a forensic scientist to conclude that I must, ergo, be a writer. And nothing else. It's such a relief, at last, to be able to put away for good the anxiety and guilt about not pursuing one of those other fantasy careers.

Now it's true that I'm not *very* old. (Though next year, when I'm sixty-six, I think I might be.) Nor am I *extremely* old. Once you start wandering haphazardly into those territories, life takes on a very different complexion, I'm sure. There is nothing to recommend being tied into an armchair in a nursing home, being fed with a spoon by someone else while pee trickles down your leg. Nor is there much fun in finding yourself wandering down an unknown street in the suburbs not knowing where you are or what your name is.

No, I am talking about Being in Your Sixties— a wonderful age, I feel, to be in.

When I reached sixty, I looked around for a book to help me through not only the joys but also the quagmires of my particular demographic. (I think that's the right word. It's a relatively new one, and I'm never quite sure how to use it. Like *diaspora*. A bit puzzling. Anyway, I'm sure you get the gist of what I mean.) When I was young, books like *Down with Skool!* by Geoffrey Willans helped me through my late school days. Then *The Catcher in the Rye* reflected my feelings during my teenage years. There was no Bridget Jones when I was a girl, but there was *Fear of Flying* by Erica Jong. And once I'd become a young mum, I often referred to books by Erma Bombeck, who wrote amusing accounts of what it was like raising a family. But then I got to sixty, and when I searched the bookshops for something entertaining and perceptive to get me through the next decade, I found nothing.

Or rather, I did find things but they were the wrong things. Books with titles like *Autumn Leaves*. Or *Golden Harvest*. One book I discovered was called *Second Youth*. Another was called *You're Only Young Twice!* What a con. I mean, being sixty has nothing at all to do with youth, however much you twist your mind to make it so. Being sixty is being sixty.

Then there was *Retiring Gracefully*.

And, by far the worst: *Armchair Aerobics*.

Now, don't get me wrong. I'm not denying that us baby boomers *are* a different kind of old than oldies from different generations. At least I think so. (Of course this may be a complete fantasy and every generation of sixty-year-olds may think that there is something special or new about them.)

But I was young in the 1960s, a world of sex, drugs, and rock 'n' roll. And I feel that my generation has a lot more in common with thirty- and forty-year-olds than with people of seventy and eighty, people who have been through World War II and suffered true hardship. And yet no matter that being a baby boomer who has gorged on sex, drugs, and rock 'n' roll in the '60s I have more in common with, say, Amy Winehouse than with a battle-scarred veteran of the First World War—the veteran and I are seen by the young as part of the same crumbling generation.

Old people are *not* all the same.

While I wouldn't want to settle down, like my grandmother at the same age, to a life of making apple pies and listening to *The Archers*, a radio soap about country folk, every night (though neither activity is something I abhor, as you will see), I can't deny that there are, inevitably, some similarities between old people of all generations. For instance, I hate staying up late. I long to leave dinner parties at 10:30 p.m. (A friend of mine has devised a new kind of way of entertaining called "Eat and Run." You ask people for drinks, give them a light supper at about eight, and expect them to have left you by 9:30–10:00 p.m. Then you have time to watch the news, clamber into a soothing bath, get into your nightgown, climb into bed, read a bit, and get to sleep by about 11:30.)

I can't really go along with those of my contemporaries who want to stay young. I don't *want* to be young anymore. It's so boring. I don't want to bicycle across Mongolia or go bungee jumping, like some of my contemporaries who feel that by showing off like this they're demonstrating how young they *really* are. I like the fact that my love affair with life is settling into comfortable companionship. People who keep pretending to be young are just pathetic specimens, the sort of folk who despise face-lifts but are, by their actions, chasing a lost youth. They are tragic failures, full of vanity, who can't come to terms with being old.

Apparently that frightful old messer-upper and confuser of human psyches, Sigmund Freud, said, "The gods are merciful when they make our lives more unpleasant as we grow old. In the end death seems less intolerable than the many burdens we have to bear." But this book is designed to outline some of the many advantages to being old. And I mean *real* advantages. We tend to dwell so much on the negative aspects of being old that we forget there is an *enormous* amount to be said for not being young anymore.

Why not take Noël Coward's view? "How foolish to think one could ever slam the door in the face of age," he said. "Much better to be polite and gracious and ask him to lunch in advance."

Though he probably said "luncheon."

I'm old enough to remember *that*.

1. Ailments

Botox and nose drops and needles for knitting,
Walkers and handrails and new dental fittings,
Bundles of magazines tied up in string,
These are a few of my favorite things.

Cadillacs and cataracts, hearing aids and glasses,
Polident and Fixodent and false teeth in glasses,
Pacemakers, golf carts, and porches with swings,
These are a few of my favorite things.

When the pipes leak, when the bones creak,
When the knees go bad,
I simply remember my favorite things,
And then I don't feel so bad.

Hot tea and crumpets and corn pads for bunions,
No spicy hot food or food cooked with onions,
Bathrobes and heating pads and hot meals
        they bring,
These are a few of my favorite things.

Back pain, confused brains, and no need
        for sinnin',
Thin bones and fractures and hair that is thinnin',
And we won't mention our short shrunken frames,
When we remember our favorite things.

When the joints ache, when the hips break,
When the eyes grow dim,
Then I remember the great life I've had,
And then I don't feel so bad.

THIS IS THE SONG that Julie Andrews sang on her birthday for the benefit of AARP—the applause at the end lasted four minutes.

When I was a young mum I would spend hours wittering on to other mums about diapers and bottle-feeding. Was breast best? Should we use disposables? I found both topics utterly gripping and could spend entire days droning on about them. Later came another subject, of interest only to people of my age with similar-aged children. Schools. I just had to hear the words *Montessori* and *public or private* and *exam results* and I'd be off (see "Boring for Britain").

Now, however, the words *diapers* or *schools* only have to be uttered in my presence and I am booking a plane ticket to Argentina. When you're not involved personally, the topics are just so crushingly dull.

But I have discovered a new topic of conversation that's going to keep me talking and interested. And luckily this one will last until the day I die.

Ailments.

I mean, we all have them, don't we? If you think you're actually physically in peak condition, ask yourself now, honestly: when was the last time you popped a pill? Was it days ago? Last week? Last month? Or, as is most likely, this morning?

Now when I go to a party, I don't say, "And do tell me, what do you *do?*" I say, "And do tell me—what's *wrong* with you?"

I only have to see an old gentleman sitting with a walker propped up beside him and I'm in there, settling down for a good old chat about the state of his health, what he makes of hospitals, does he think mixed wards are a good idea, does he pronounce BUPA (the British United Provident Association, which provides private health insurance) as "Byewpa" or "Booper," and what medication he's on. And, most important, if he's had an operation, which surgeon did it, and was he any good.

I only have to hear the word *pills* whispered across the room at a party, and, with the speed of a character from a Warner Bros. cartoon, I've joined the group and started to discuss the merits and demerits of glucosamine sulphate and fish oil and whatever else is on the agenda. "Does *your* health authority send you a do-it-yourself bowel cancer test now that you're sixty? Well, mine doesn't—but I *do* get free flu shots. . . ."

Someone started telling me about her bad back the other day and then, halfway through the most fascinating story about discs and bone degeneration, she suddenly broke off apologetically, saying she must be boring me. "Boring me?" I said. "Not at all. What else would we be talking about? The state of the Middle East? Will the Internet mean the end of books as we know them? Those topics aren't for me. Big yawn. You had got, I think, to the fifth vertebra going north to south down the spine. Pray continue. I am all ears."

(Speaking of which . . . but more about ears later.)

These days, the best conversation of all is what a friend of my mother's used to call an "organ recital." Here are some topics to get you going.

Digestion

Hands up, those of you who have spent nights white with terror wondering if a) you have cancer of the esophagus or b) heart problems. And whose anxieties were triggered either by a burning feeling in your throat or an indigestiony feeling in your chest.

And how many, I wonder, have discovered that the answer was simply *acid reflux?* This is something to do with some valve failing to work properly, which means that the acid in your stomach seeps up to your gullet during the night, and it's easily controlled with a pill. Yes, I know that another way of controlling it is to drink less but, in my case at least, this is simply not an option.

Feet

I suppose at one time or other *all* our feet were soft, dimpled, pudgy things with toes like tiny buds, and soles as soft as velvet. It seems incredible that such delicate little paws, warm objects just made for kissing, could possibly turn into the two gnarled, horned bits of driftwood, underpinned by what seems like beef jerky, which we find sticking out from our ankles when we get old. Mine have developed grotesque bunions and yellowing nails that are more in need of trimming with a chainsaw than a pair of nail clippers. What makes it all extra unpleasant is that while feet appear to be hoary objects, protected by hard skin and corns, they become, as we get older, extra sensitive. Sometimes just walking up the street is, for me, absolute agony—unless, of course, I am wearing a pair of shoes or sneakers so ugly that I need to put a paper bag over my head before I can even leave the house.

It's gotten to the point where my feet are so painful that I'm starting to wonder whether it wouldn't be worth risking the lives of a few blind people, rather than force the entire older generation to wince with agony as they step, at every pedestrian crossing, onto a surface covered in those large bumpy dots, like giant Braille.

After a really long walk, far from feeling full of zip and buzz, I have to put my feet into a bowl of cool water, not only to ease the pain but also to reduce the size of my disgustingly swollen ankles.

When I was young I never thought that the expression "Oh my poor feet" would ever escape my lips, but now I'm never really happy unless my feet are up—and I mean *up,* not just plonked on the ground, as they are when I sit.

This pain means that before you know where you are you feel that you need to be shod, rather like a horse, and often you can end up visiting a private podiatrist. He can not only relieve your feet, but also your wallet, of hundreds of dollars, just to create some kind of orthotic, a curved piece of material to put in your shoes to raise your arches (which you can get just as easily from a good drugstore for a couple of dollars).

And have you noticed that walking itself has become more difficult? I'm five foot seven and I was horrified to find a smaller, younger friend with stubby little legs managing, for some inexplicable reason, to walk much faster than me. Even with my longer legs and apparently bigger strides, I still lag behind. Weird.

Addictions

I have come across some poor people as old as eighty whose doctors refuse to prescribe them tranquilizers or sleeping pills on the grounds that they "might become addicted." Now, it's understandable that you wouldn't want to be responsible for putting a person of twenty on a regimen that might result in their dependence on Mother's Little Helpers for the rest of their lives, but at sixty or seventy? Why not? The minute I know that I've only got months to live, the first thing I'm going to do is to take up smoking again. Indeed, in some tolerant hospices, they even provide smoking rooms for patients, so when eventually you get carted off to what your relatives kindly call "another hospital" remember this. By finding out if it has a smoking room you will be able to ascertain whether you're going to the place to be cured— or to die.

As Kingsley Amis said, "There is no pleasure I could be induced to forgo by the prospect of two extra years in a nursing home."

I'm also looking forward to being able to start knocking back the G-and-Ts at ten in the morning, without a shadow of guilt.

Talking to Yourself

This is a great new pleasure if you've never talked to yourself before. "Hello," you can say

26

to yourself. "Sorry about not being in touch for so long. But I can let bygones be bygones if you can."

Talking to yourself involves, often, a constant commentary on life. "I'm going to get my spectacles . . . now where did I put them . . . spectacles, spectacles . . . I must have put them somewhere. Pity I can't see well enough to find them. I couldn't have put them on my head, could I? . . . Like those awful models . . . models, models, why was I thinking of models? . . . Now what was I looking for? Oh dear me, oh dear me . . ."

On your own you can conduct murderous—but utterly harmless—arguments with imaginary other people. "How dare you imply that I'm too old to drive! I'll show you! You stand in front of the car, and I'll get into the car, and you tell me my eyesight's not good enough to mow you down with a single rev!"

Drugs

Don't you just *love* them? At one point I took so many of them that I had to buy one of those strange gadgets from a pharmacy with little compartments with Monday, Tuesday, Wednesday, et cetera written on them. Even then, the boxes

weren't big enough to accommodate the vast drugstore of tablets that I consumed each morning. One of the problems is, of course, that these days, being old, we in Britain are in the lucky position of being able to get our prescriptions absolutely free. I never go to the doctor without coming away with a free prescription, which I take eagerly to the pharmacist to cash in. I can barely resist waving my pills at every passing under-sixty-year-old and saying, in a gloating voice, "Look at these pills! They're free! All free! And they're mine! Because I'm older than you! Nah nah nah-*nah* nah!"

Warfarin. Statins. Beta-blockers . . . small doses of aspirin . . . vitamin supplements . . . arthritis pills . . . calcium . . . zinc . . . milk thistle to cope with my overworked liver. I take seven pills, every morning.

Oh, and fish oil of course. In fact I take so much fish oil I'm thinking of joining an aquarium.

Speaking of drugs, though, what about the other sort of drugs? You know, the illegal ones. The ones that you "do"? (Funny how you never "do" glucosamine sulphate. You just "do" cocaine, dope, heroin, etc.)

I used to, in the '60s, try the odd drug. I smoked a lot of dope, snorted a bit of cocaine, and even smoked heroin once (well, didn't we all? Oh, sorry, perhaps we didn't), but Ecstasy hadn't been invented then and I never dared try LSD in case I went bonkers.

Now we're all going bonkers anyway, perhaps this is just the moment to try them—not to mention crack cocaine, ketamine, and that weird South American jungle drug, ayahuasca, which apparently introduces you to God. Actually, I'm still a teensy-weensy bit scared of that experience, so I think I'll try that when I'm seventy.

PS: Just read in the paper that a seventy-seven-year-old grandmother was jailed for trying to smuggle $1 million of cocaine into Britain. Oh, what larks lie ahead.

Anxiety

Lots of my friends no longer dare to drive on highways. Single women who hitched across the Gobi Desert when they were thirty and who, in their forties, drove across India and America in cars piled high with small children, now find that, faced with a highway, they are reduced to quivering Jell-O.

And when I was young I couldn't understand why my grandmother always wanted us to be at the train station what seemed like hours before the train. Now I behave exactly like her. I get the suitcase out from under the stairs about a week before I go away, and start packing in a desultory way. Spare pills, extra pairs of glasses, bottle

29

opener, and quarter bottle of brandy just in case my hosts turn out to be the sort of people who unlock the drinks cabinet only after 8:00 p.m. Or, worse, don't even drink. Nail clippers, blow-dryer, Band-Aids (just in case), bunion splint, spare hankies (see Drips under Runny Nose, later) . . . the suitcase is pretty much full by the time I start packing in earnest, two days before I'm due to leave.

Every older person I know gets into a total panic before they go away. They're unable to sleep and have to leave trails of notes for who-ever's left at home, with foreign phone numbers, emergency numbers of neighbors, burglar alarms, rules about security procedures. . . . My whole rationale these days is one of "Better safe than sorry!" and "Just in case!"

Some oldies, I gather, even buy portable bath handles that somehow stick onto strange bath-room walls, just in case they can't get easily out of the bath. And speaking of baths, when did you first get a rubber mat to put at the bottom of the bathtub to stop you slipping? I've got one. It's blue and covered with raised patterns of dolphins and starfish.

Recently, my grandson came over and, to my —and his—dismay, discovered that the back was alive with a slimy black mold. (It reminded me of the day I was looking for a saucepan in my own grandmother's house and came across one with the remains of scrambled egg still dried on inside. I felt sick.) I dare you to look underneath yours. Go on!

Balance
Why you should fall over more often when you're old than when you're young is a mystery to me. But unless you do, as I do, constant exercises that involve your standing on one leg like a flamingo for minutes at a stretch each morning, you may find you have a tendency to stumble in the street and evoke in your companions an unwelcome hand hovering under your elbow for the rest of the journey. If it's a man, he will probably take your upper arm in a painful grip, and try to steer you across the street as if you were a recalcitrant supermarket cart.

Sleep
Well, sleep after sixty is all gone to pot, isn't it? I've taken, sometimes, to having a snooze in the afternoon. And that means that although I can fall asleep at night straight away, I often wake, riven by panic about why I was born and whether death will be quite as jolly as I usually predict it will, at about four in the morning. I used to put on the BBC World Service and be comforted by interviews with Morris dancers, or documentaries about raffia-making in the Congo, but ever since it got political I now risk hearing about

child abduction in China and boy soldiers who are forced to perform clitorectomies on their AIDS-ridden mothers—all very upsetting. I don't find relief from the radio anymore. Sometimes reading a P. G. Wodehouse book will help. But I usually take a quarter of a Temazepam (Free! Free! All free!) and knock myself out.

Don't you think it would be a good idea if someone invented a kind of map, rather like those you used to find on the Paris Metro system, whereby certain spots lit up when you pressed a button? Only in this case it would show you which of your friends were awake and panicking in the early hours. Then we could call each other up and chat reassuringly till dawn.

Failing this I have been known, before I go to sleep, to write, in a large felt-tipped pen on a piece of paper, "Virginia! It is the middle of the night! Stop worrying! It will all be all right in the morning!" and leave it on my bedside table. When I wake in the night, gibbering with anxiety, this message can often do something to calm me down.

Arthritis and Mobility

Every morning I get out of bed and I have to hobble to the lavatory. However restless I have been all night, I just feel seized up. It takes breakfast and a hot bath to unglue my joints. And if anyone suggests I go to a gym, I'm immediately reminded of the old joke which goes: "I was feeling old and out of shape, so I joined an aerobics class for the over-fifties. I twisted, gyrated, jumped up and down and perspired for an hour. But by the time I got my leotard on, the class was over."

Recently I actually bought myself a cane. Me! A *cane!* In the '60s I used to write a rock column for the *Daily Mail* and interview the likes of Mick Jagger and the Beatles and be asked about why I wore my skirts so short. I was often consulted as a professional "young person." Now I'm called up whenever any newspaper wants a quote on grannies or Alzheimer's disease or the plight of retirees' bunions. Now I give talks to the Colostomy Association and use my cane when I leave just in case I fall over, my balance —despite the flamingo-standing exercises—not being quite as good as it used to be. (Does Mick have these issues, I wonder?)

Even putting on clothes can be a bit of a struggle. Have you ever gotten into a dress you just can't get out of? (I'm addressing women here, obviously—or maybe not so obviously.) Recently I managed to wriggle my way into one, but when I needed to take it off, I just couldn't force my arms sufficiently far to put them over my head and bend them downward, to pull the whole thing off. I had to get some scissors and carefully unpick a seam before I could escape.

Then there's putting on tights . . . I use the sitting-on-a-bed-and-then-rolling-back-like-a-hedgehog method, with my legs in the air before I pull the tights down. Pulling *down* seems, these days, to be easier than pulling *up*.

At least I can still, just, put on my shoes.

And I can still, just, sit on the floor. Though getting up is another matter. As for kneeling to do a jigsaw puzzle with a grandchild—ouch! What *does* happen to your knees when you age?

And although I haven't actually ordered my Stannah Stairlift, I am starting to consider the options.

So far I haven't yet lost any height. People always say, when they meet their former nannies or teachers, that they hadn't realized they were so tiny. But they have almost certainly shrunk an inch or two. I wonder if there'll come a time when we say to each other, "Oh, I remember you were *this* high!" But this time, rather than bending down to indicate two feet from the ground, we'll be reaching on tiptoe to show six feet or so.

And no, I've never had to use a walker. Yet. I take consolation from a friend who had to use one. She dyed what was left of her hair purple, and decorated her walker with flashing pink lights—keeping the battery in her pocket—with spectacular results.

Sight

Having been nearsighted all my life I'm one of the lucky ones who can now only read *without* my glasses—another old-age perk. But most of my friends can't order a meal in a restaurant without putting on their specs. As one said, "Not only do I have to put on my glasses to read the menu, I need them to be introduced to my dinner as well!"

But because people of sixty need two-thirds more light to read by than they did when they were twenty, the real problem is the dark. Have you noticed how dark your bedroom and living room have become recently? It's not because the bulbs have got dimmer, it's because you just can't see as well as you used to. Most old people hate driving in the dark. And as for going to see shows in museums—forget it. With the obsession for preserving the colors of fabrics and water-colors, most of us over sixty, when we're visiting an exhibition of fashion or paintings, need not only the big print catalog but also a powerful flashlight.

Apart from macular degeneration and cataracts, which may well come to us all, the most irritating thing about getting old is the presence of those wretched little black ants that sail across your vision—floaters. These are the common cold of the eye, in that no one can do anything about them (well, they can, but the operation is dangerous). My reading gets faster and faster over the years as I try desperately to read ahead of the floater waiting, a millisecond behind my reading, to obliterate the page.

Cancer
So many of my friends have cancer, or have survived cancer, or have friends and relatives dying of cancer that, while I used to wake up in the middle of the night in a cold sweat saying to myself, "Help, I think I've got cancer!" now I wake in the night in a cold sweat saying to myself, "Oh no, I *haven't* got cancer! There must be something wrong with me!"

Doctors
The big dilemma about doctors, when you get older, is which kind to choose—young or old. The old ones have more experience, so you're in safer hands. But the young ones have more up-to-date knowledge. Whatever the answer is, we're now at an age when we actually do know our own bodies pretty well—probably better than most doctors of any age. After all, we've lived with our bodies for over sixty years. We know the difference between cystitis and something more threatening. We don't panic any more when we get the flu. And if some youngster of a medic dares suggest that the agonizing pain we feel in our knee is psychosomatic, we do have the sense

to suggest that the doctor refer us for an X ray, just in case it's not.

Sometimes I wish I weren't too old to train as a doctor because, like most old people, I know quite a lot about various kinds of medicine, having experienced a variety of illnesses over the years. Quite a few friends consult me in my self-elected role as Dr. Ironside; I'm pleased to report that I've already saved at least one life and, by my sophisticated diagnosing techniques, have certainly put a couple of friends on the path to symptom-free lives.

Dozing

Dozing is, you might say, hardly an ailment, but a physical joy that comes with old age. I've never dozed in my life until now. And it is the most pleasant sensation. You lie on a sofa, watching television or reading a book. And then you feel as if there were an invisible hypnotist in the room, willing you to close your eyes. You feel sleep stealing over, you feel your book flopping onto your nose, and before you know where you are you are off on a wonderful afternoon doze, probably, I'm afraid to say, with your mouth open. But what *pleasure*.

If I have something important to do in the afternoon, I am wary of having any kind of lunch. In fact I only have to have a glass of orange juice and a *poppadom* and afterward I feel like a hero in a film who has been slipped a Mickey by an evil enemy. The room goes all wobbly, I start seeing double, and before I know it, I'm collapsed on the sofa, out for the count for a good half hour.

Another odd thing is that when you rise from your doze to make yourself a restorative cup of tea and grab a much-needed digestive biscuit (again, something I never used to do), you get up by placing your hands on the arms of your chair and kind of hoisting yourself up while, from your lips, escapes the undignified sound *"Ugh!"*—a grunt every bit as powerful and involuntary as those grunting servers at Wimbledon.

Hearing

I went for a hearing test the other day. They're starting to become as commonplace as eye tests. And although I can't hear anything that anyone says to me at a noisy party, my hearing isn't nearly as bad as I thought. Quite normal "for my age"—one of those phrases we'll be hearing (or not hearing as the case may be) a lot more in the future.

I am starting to judge a restaurant not primarily on the quality of its food but on the quality of its acoustics. I only really like restaurants that have carpeting on the floor—and preferably on the ceiling and walls, too—so I'm a great fan of the stained carpets and flocked wallpaper in Indian restaurants that are, sadly, being phased out to make way for white walls and tiled floors. The more cloth napkins, tablecloths, and general muffling material, the better for us hard of hearing . . . it sucks up all the sound of other diners. Otherwise I often find the whole table of oldies cocking their heads as they listen, as if they're trying to tune in to a special radio wavelength that will make comprehension easier.

And at last I have discovered what is meant by "my good ear."

Funny Turns

A couple of my friends recently have had what can only be called "funny turns." One was found lying by the side of her bed, briefly unconscious; the other had been cleaning windows when he was found, again briefly unconscious, having fallen off a chair. No one knew what on earth was going on, but it seems this is a pretty common condition among older people, known in medical terms as "the Drop." Maddeningly, however many ladders I climb to change the bulbs in the overhead lights, or however many stairs I tumble down, drugged with Temazepam on my way to the loo in the middle of the night, I haven't been able to experience one of these interesting markers. Yet.

Runny Nose

Where do these drips come from? I never had them when I was young. But I think I may have the answer. Do you remember a comic strip called *Georgie's Germs*, when you were young? It featured a young boy, George, and little goblins were depicted inside his body, pumping his heart with bellows, punching out red spots when he had measles, adding gunpowder to special concoctions to make a sneeze. Do you think they're all still in there, these tiny people, manufacturing nose drips for when we're old? Waiting for awkward moments to release them? Just as you're kissing your hostess goodnight.

I asked someone the way when I was lost in the country the other day, and this old farmer stuck his head through the window, and on the end of his nose was a drip just waiting to fall. "You first turn to the left," he said. . . . "Then the right . . . then round the roundabout . . ." And I kept praying the thing wouldn't launch itself into my car. Or my face. Teaming up with my own drip.

Skin

Lots of funny things happen to your skin when you're old. Not only do you get freckles on your hands—mine look just like my own grandmother's and I find it utterly unnerving looking down and seeing *her* hands wiggling about at the end of my wrists—but your hair gets surprisingly thin everywhere except in your nose and, sometimes, your chin. I have one weird black hair that grows from my chin like that of a witch in a fairy tale. Then your body gets covered with tiny little red lines—thread veins. Thread veins if you're lucky. Otherwise you look down and find you are covered with great fat pulsing purple rivers—varicose veins. They haven't hit me yet but the moment I find one I'm going to get it stripped out, pronto.

Two fun things to do with your old skin: one is to cut off those funny little skin tags you get, with a pair of scissors—very fun. And the other is to pinch the flesh all over your upper arms so that you are covered with little bits of skinny peaks, rather like an iced Christmas cake. This is surprisingly satisfying—though not to onlookers.

Tests

I just *love* medical tests. Now that there's not a man to pay regular attention to my body, I have to settle for lying back in a luxurious chair and savoring the pleasurable feeling of blood being drained out of my arm by a good-looking male nurse, ideally from Sri Lanka. Or indulge myself with the blissful relaxation of a bone scan, while a great machine thrums its way over my entire body. I wasn't too keen on the heart test, which I had when I was so frightened I was having a heart attack (yes, the usual old acid-reflux scare), but in the end it was good fun.

"How much exercise do you get?" asked the doctor.

"None," I replied briskly.

"Then how breathless do you get," he said, coldly, unfazed, "when you run for a bus?" Using my Lady Bracknell voice, I told him in no uncertain terms that I *never* ran for a bus. I told him that the only way to catch a bus was to miss the one before. I usually drove everywhere, and did he know that if I went on a bus I got it free, unlike him because he was too young nah nah nah-*nah*-nah et cetera (see earlier).

In an attempt to establish his superiority, he got me onto a treadmill, saying that even fit young men lasted no longer than eleven minutes.

Don't ask me how, but I managed to do *twelve*. Admittedly I had to go to bed for a week afterward, but it was worth it, just to see the look on his pink young face.

Alternative Medicine

Along with the topic of mugging, this is a subject of discussion that is banned from my house. I do not spend hours and hours in the kitchen slaving over pheasant *à la Normande* for eight people in order for it to be eaten to the accompaniment of airheaded talk about whether acupuncture works or not, or how wonderful arnica and echinacea are. I've read enough books on quack medicine to be completely convinced that the bad press given to alternative medicine is, by and large, entirely justified. I'm quite prepared to believe in their placebo powers, but do I really want to hear about the miraculous effect that Bach Flower Remedies had on some godchild's asthma, or how my friend's husband's brother-in-law's tennis elbow was cured with a diet of dock-leaf soup? No, I do not.

My Personal Story

I'm *so* glad you asked. I thought you'd never get around to it. Well, I *have* been feeling a bit old recently. It's called "senioritis," I think. I suppose it's having had this wretched colon-removing operation so recently. (No, not cancer, but thank you for asking.) A much older friend of mine said, wisely, that when you get older and have a setback like a Big Operation, you do recover, like everyone else, but you can never recover completely. You fall a few ratchets when you're ill, but when you recover you're always one ratchet down from where you started. I know what he means. Hence the word *ratchety*, no doubt. Or do I mean *crotchety?*

Yes, I actually sport a colostomy bag. It's not too bad, honestly. Apparently R. J. Mitchell had one—the chap who invented the Spitfire. I always imagine his bag was rather leathery, covered with metal studs, like his flying helmet. And, oddly, Henri Matisse had one, too. Can't imagine what *his* looked like. Now, many people have trouble finding something positive to say about having a colostomy bag, but it does mean you'll never get rectal cancer. And it does give you complete control, even when you have diarrhea. And certainly when you are on a country walk and need to "go" you don't have to scrabble around for dried-up leaves to wipe your bottom with. Every cloud, as they say . . .

When I was writing a piece about having a colostomy bag for the editor of a magazine for the older generation, she shrieked, "A colostomy bag? How cool can you get? Have you got shoes to go with it?"

Ailments as Excuses

Don't forget that ailments are great for wriggling out of things you don't want to do. Never be specific. Just say a phrase that you could *never* have used when you were young: "I'm so sorry I can't come. I've had a recurrence of the old trouble."

2. Memory

There is a wicked inclination in most people to suppose an old man is decayed in his intellects. If a young or middle-aged man, when leaving a company, does not recollect where he laid his hat, it is nothing; but if the same inattention is discovered in an old man, people will shrug up their shoulders and say, "His memory is going."

—Dr. Johnson

BARELY A DAY GOES BY without some ancient contemporary moaning to me, "Oh, my memory's going! We're all getting Alzheimer's!"

Instead of rejoicing in the wonderful *changes* that happen to our memories as we age, these ancient Cassandras simply bewail the fact that they can't remember the name of a film that usually no one in their right minds can remember anyway.

"Oh, it was that film, you know the one, with the airplane in it, *British* something or was it *English* . . . with that actor Ralph . . . his last name starts with *F* I think, and it's got two words . . . oh, what's his name? Ralph Harris? No that's the singer. . . . It sounds like 'the *dah*-dah *dah*-dah. . . .' "

They can blather on for hours, pulling out all the drawers in their brains, emptying them in front of me, and scrabbling through them while I stand by saying, "I couldn't care less. I can't remember the name of the film because it wasn't important and frankly wasn't worth remembering. I know the film you mean . . . just get on with your wretched story . . . !"

When they finally give up on the name, they stop and, with a sheepish smile, say, "Ah—we're all losing our memories . . . a Senior Moment!" (or, as a more amusing friend calls it, a CRAFT Moment—"Can't Remember a Fucking Thing").

But just because I forget something it doesn't mean anything at all. It's usually because I've quite simply forgotten something. Like I sometimes forgot to take my pencil case to school. To be frank, I've never had much of a memory anyway. I've never had a memory to lose. When I was fourteen I used to go into a room wondering what I'd come to get, and no doubt even at two I was probably staggering up the stairs to my bedroom and completely forgetting that it was my teddy bear I was seeking.

If, when I was young, I forgot the date of the Battle of Hastings, I didn't go on to my fellow pupils about how we were all losing our memories. I just said, like a normal person, "I've forgotten." (Anyway, I hate being bracketed with everyone else as a doddery old fool. It's like when people rather older than oneself—or, come to that, younger—start a sentence with the phrase "Well, at *our* age . . ." And you feel like tweaking their nose and saying, "Excuse me, could you rephrase that?")

Apparently there are three stages to memory: Acquisition, Storage, and Retrieval, and as we age, the capacity to carry out the processes can vary, person to person. The one that worries most people after middle age is Retrieval. Life seems to be one long quest. "Where did I put my glasses?" "Where did I leave my bag?" "What happened to that last bit of cookie that I'm sure I didn't finish—or did I? My awaiting taste buds and saliva tell me I didn't." When we scrabble around for the names of books, actors, or even our closest friends, it feels as if we are riffling through old Dickensian card files, the corners of which are grimy and rounded with age, while the young are simply leaping through their memory systems as neatly and swiftly as brand-new state-of-the-art computers.

(These days I sometimes get so irritated by failing to remember where I put things that I think I ought to carry a small tape recorder with easily accessible buttons that, when pressed, would respond with the words, "Oh, where's my bag?" "Where did I leave my glasses?" "Have you seen my phone?" simply to save my voice unnecessary stress. But I comfort myself with the fact that I get so much exercise running up- and downstairs hunting for them that I certainly don't need to go to the gym.)

But is all this memory stuff really such a big deal?

Cathryn Jakobson Ramin—who wrote a book with the snappy title *That Memory Book: How to Deal with Distractibility, Forgetfulness and Other Unnerving High Jinks of the Middle-Aged Brain*—embarked on a quest to improve her memory. Eschewing the dreary old mnemonics —why should she have to imagine, whenever she went to the shops, a dog being ridden by a pig holding a bag, for example when she wanted to buy pet food, sausages, and tea?—she ventured into the medical world. She consulted neurologists and biologists, and made forays into the realms of meditation, neurofeedback, and anything else she could lay her hands on. Were her cortisol levels too high? Anxiety can cause lack of memory. Was she eating properly? Fish oil can improve memory. Had she had a head injury when young? Was it a hormonal problem? Could it be her hippocampus? Or her thyroid?

Too much alcohol? Not enough? Would play-ing bridge help? What about Sudoku? Did her synapses play a part?

But in the end nothing particularly made much difference and she just had to come to terms with the situation. And make lists. And there is nothing wrong with that. I've been making lists since I was ten. Admittedly they've changed slightly from the old days when they featured items like "Feed cat," "Do homework," "Have bath," "Write thank-you letter to Granny." But they are still very useful. (I hate to admit it, but today I hadn't written "Have bath" on the list so after I'd had it I actually wrote in the words "Have bath" and immediately, triumphantly, crossed it out.)

I don't want to trivialize true memory loss, of course. There is a moment when it's worth seeking help. "Where did I leave my glasses?" is one thing, but "What are glasses?" is another. Losing your car keys is one thing; losing your ability to drive is another. Forgetting your granddaughter's name is one thing; forgetting to pick her up from school is another.

When a friend said to me the other day that she was losing her memory and it was worrying her so much she'd made an appointment to see the ". . . what is that person called . . . you know, the one you go to when you're not feeling well?" I realized she really was getting quite seriously wonky as far as her memory went.

But unless you have serious memory problems there is a lot to be said for changing memory patterns. They don't change, necessarily, for the worse. Indeed if you're anything like me, they change for the *better*.

As I get older, it's true, I often can't remember in the morning whether I've taken one of my seven pills (Free! All free!) or not. And I'm *frequently* forgetting where on earth I parked my car (sometimes I think I should leave a trail of crumbs, like Hansel and Gretel did, to retrace their steps in the woods), but there are all kinds of perks to our new memory patterns. Honestly.

Joy of Forgetting Plots

For a start, there's the joy of forgetting quite a lot of useless things. These days, rather than wade through new novels that nine times out of ten I'll throw across the room with rage and boredom long before I get to the end, I simply stick with the old favorites. The other day I reread *Anna Karenina* with enormous pleasure, and recently I seized on a republication of a favorite author, Patrick Hamilton, thinking it was one I'd never read, thoroughly enjoyed it and, when I put it into the Hamilton section of my bookcase (yes, I have one), found that I already had a copy that I had certainly read before. Then I know I watched the Bette Davis film *All About Eve* about thirty years ago when black-and-white movies were a staple on TV. And I remembered the odd scene. But I couldn't remember the plot and the whole thing, upon seeing it again (though it felt as if it were for the first time), gave me a real thrill. *Battleship Potemkin* was another huge surprise and joy, even though my father took me to see it at the National Film Theatre when I was about fourteen. I have become a glutton for old black-and-white movies that I enjoyed at the time, like *Victim* and *The Servant*, not to mention *On the Waterfront*, which not only knock the socks off modern films but also, since I can't remember anything about them, strike me as extraordinarily new and fresh.

Joy of Forgetting Pain

Though we tend to remember emotional rather than physical pain, I've forgotten quite how depressed I used to be, which is a relief. I've forgotten the '60s, thank God (they say "If you remember the '60s you weren't there," but I know my kind of forgetting is the equivalent of the forgetting of a dreadful trauma), and I've forgotten an enormous number of the ghastly men I ended up in bed with. Indeed, a puffy old alcoholic with a beer belly and a gray ponytail oiled up to me the other day in a club and breathed, "I remember your beautiful body,

Virginia. . . ." and I was able to reply, with shattering conviction to anyone within earshot, "Well, I can tell you, I don't remember yours!" "Darling!" I added for good measure. Because it was true. I couldn't. Thank God.

Joy of Forgetting Useless Facts

It must be awful for some men to forget facts, such as whether Napoleon was exiled to Elba in 1814 or 1815 (men, because of their brain makeup, have a tendency to collect and retain more facts than women; hence the large number of male, and small number of female, memory artists and savants). But there is some consolation.

Who really wants to be like those rare people who can remember everything and whose minds are like those disgusting rooms that American ladies on TV, with the aid of several bonfires, are employed to declutter? In extreme cases these information hoarders can't even operate normal lives, because their brains are just so stuffed with junk and they're so busy remembering everything.

There's a wonderful passage in Conan Doyle's *A Study in Scarlet* that tells of Sherlock Holmes's amazement when told by Dr. Watson that the earth revolves around the sun. Holmes had never known this fact and was determined, once he did know, to forget it. " 'You see,' he explained,

'I consider that a man's brain originally is like a little empty attic, and you have to stock it with such furniture as you choose. A fool takes in all the lumber of every sort that he comes across . . . You say that we go round the sun. If we went round the moon it would not make a penny-worth of difference to me or my work.' "

Pleasure of Long-term Memory

Another plus of our new memory systems is that, although we may lose capacity in our short-term memory, our long-term memory often seems, oddly, to improve. These days, cracks seem to appear in the walls of my consciousness, revealing glimpses of the past as clear as if they were happening in front of my eyes. Sometimes I feel intense emotions about these moments that I never experienced at the time.

I recently had a very odd moment in a carpet shop. I was flicking through samples and suddenly came across a brown square that was exactly the same color as an old coat my father used to wear. For a few seconds I was transported back to being a little girl, holding him by the hand. I could smell him, hear his voice, almost feel his cuff on my wrist. I was filled with an odd, poignant mixture of comfort and nostalgia. And then last week I saw a piece of graph paper in a French supermarket, and I was instantly back at my schoolroom desk, drawing graphs for the math teacher. The tears that sprang to my eyes were inexplicably pleasurable. I only have to smell the whiff of a bonfire and I'm immediately flung back into my grandparents' garden in Herefordshire, standing shyly by, in the setting sun, as my grandfather potters around me, occasionally poking the fire with a stick.

Brand-new Memories
Memories can be like old photocopies, fading with time, and distorting and degrading every time they're remembered anew. Sometimes these memories, created by constant remembering, are almost better than the original ones.

The Plus of a Huge Past
And we mustn't forget that we oldies have a past. That's something that no young person has. We have acres and acres, field upon field of experience, contact with different people from all walks of life. Our pasts are like caves of treasure, in which we can wander at our leisure, with the special bonus of not actually having to experience any of it ever again.

The Problem with Names
Now, the thing that most of my friends hate particularly about their memories' changing patterns is that they forget names. But apparently we forget names only because they don't actually

mean anything. And anyway, there's a simple solution. If we're stymied at a party when a friend, whose name we've forgotten, comes up to us when we're talking to someone else, we can easily just say (having primed the first friend to stick out her hand and say her name on meeting the other person), "Do you two know each other?" The person whose name you've forgotten will automatically say her own name in reply to your friend telling her hers.

Another, less insulting, way of admitting you've forgotten someone's name when you're introducing them is to feign complete blankness. "Wow, I suddenly feel I've had a blackout! I can't remember *either* of your names! Senior Moment!" (This is where the use of the phrase "Senior Moment" *does* come in useful.) If I'm feeling too shy to say, as I should, "I'm so sorry, but I've just forgotten your name," I always use a sly trick and say, warmly, "Oh dear, I've forgotten your name . . . all I remember is that I know I like you!"

The other infallible way of getting the conversation going with someone whose name you can't remember is the simple, "How lovely to see you. And how is the old problem?"

Memory Tricks

When you forget words, there's always the "sounds like" trick or the Alphabet Trick, in

55

which you simply trawl down the alphabet until you reach the right letter and miraculously the word you want springs into your mind. The other day I was having lunch with someone and we were talking about making our own picture frames. I mentioned that at home I'd gotten a "thing that you use to make a frame . . . it's made out of metal. . . ." She was baffled. "I'll remember by the end of the meal," I said, wisely putting the whole thing aside so that my slow retrieval system could get going. I did a quick trawl down the alphabet to give the system a boost. Sure enough, in the middle of coffee, I suddenly found myself yelling, "Miter!" much to her—and my—surprise. And, indeed, to the surprise of the whole restaurant.

Too Old to Care?

Perhaps because I'm less anxious, now that I'm older, my own memory seems to be slightly improving. But, fundamentally, I'm pretty relaxed about memory—losing it or keeping it. So what if I walk into a room and can't remember what I've come in for? It'll come to me. So what if I can't remember the name of the actress who played in that film, you know, the one about boiled rabbits? Who cares?

And isn't one of the reasons we don't remember so much that our brains are already absolutely bursting with information? As Homer Simpson, a wise old bird, says, "Every time I learn something new, it pushes something old out of my brain."

If you look into my mind, you'll find a lovely, dusty Victorian drawing room, crammed with stuffed birds, spider plants, bits of shells, old crockery, piles of dusty books, pictures. . . . Look into a young person's mind and you'll discover it looks like one of those grim, bleak, white minimalist rooms you see in interior decorating magazines. Stylish, but almost empty. No wonder a young person can remember everything. They've got nothing to remember. (And yes, I do know I've said something like this before. I've just *chosen* to repeat it, so there.)

Of course I get annoyed when someone leaves a message on my answering machine, giving their cell-phone number so quickly I can never write it down fast enough to get it in one shot. Often I will have to listen to a lengthy message again and again just to get the full number.

And it does irritate me that although when speaking I rarely use the wrong word, I find that my fingers can sometimes fail me when writing. For instance, when typing the word *irritate* above, I inadvertently typed the word *imitate* instead.

Quite honestly I prefer my memory as it is now, compared with how it used to be. Most of the things I forget are things I would really hate to remember. Anyway, who needs memory? Again and again I can't help feeling we are the luckiest generation alive. Just as we are starting to lose our memories, what happens?

Along comes Wikipedia.

3. Confidence

I'm a big girl now, mummy,
I can walk, holding on to a chair,
   and I can feed myself with a spoon
   and I can say "Moo."

I'm a big girl now, mummy,
   I can go to school
   and I can cross the road *all by myself.*

I'm a big girl now, mummy,
And I can come back home at whatever
      time I *like,*
   You're bloody lucky I come home at all!

I'm a big girl now, mummy,
I sit on committees
   and boss other people around
   and lay down the rules about what you
      give my children to eat if I let them
stay with you.

I'm a big girl now, mummy,
   And now I can face death calmly.

And then we will meet again.
   Mummy.

I WAS ONE of those children who screamed with panic whenever my mother threatened to take me to a party. I'd suck my thumb in a corner, cling to her skirts in terror. Usually she left and I'd be the child hanging about with other people's grandparents, refusing to play statues or musical chairs, and, when it came to teatime, shaking my head silently when offered a pink cupcake and refusing to sit at the table with others. The only thing I could whisper was, "Is it time to go home?" Or "When is my mummy coming?"

My reports at school had me down as a child who needed to "come out of her shell" and the prospect of spending the night even with a close relative reduced me to tears of panic. When I was about seven years old, I once went to stay with a school friend who lived across the street. From her window I could see my parents' bedroom. When, at about nine thirty, I looked out of the window and saw my parents moving around, I felt so homesick and became so hysterical that I had to be chaperoned back across the street, tears pouring down my face, holding the little suitcase I'd so carefully packed that morning.

Shy has been my middle name . . . until now, in my sixties, I have the sort of confidence I can only describe as sickening. Okay, probably most of it's an act but, if so, it's one that could only be developed after a certain age.

It's such a relief. I can actually stand up to people. I can tell Jehovah's Witnesses who ring my bell to bugger off. I can say, when my dentist tells me I need a filling, "Hang on! Before you go ahead could you have the courtesy to explain the procedure to me? It is *my* mouth we're talking about here!" (And when he's finished, and it's all worked out nicely, I now have the confidence to kiss him on both cheeks and, using his first name, without even asking if he minds, tell him what a total genius he is.)

If I find myself at a committee meeting, I often hear a familiar voice—mine—asking a question, which is usually something along the lines of, "I didn't understand a word of that. Could you say exactly what you mean in two sentences? And in plain English please?" And suddenly I find that no one else in the room could understand it either and everyone's very pleased someone was confident enough—and old enough—to ask. Indeed, sometimes I'm almost too confident. You know that moment when you hear yourself saying something really frightful that you were thinking privately, and it just leaps out like a toad from a princess's mouth in a fairy tale? You suddenly hear yourself saying to someone who's just been to the hairdresser's and had all her locks cut off for a short bob: "Oh. But it was so pretty the *old* way you had it!" Scientists say it's something to do with your synapses atrophying in your frontal lobes as you age, but I think it's just extraordinary confidence.

I have started, in my sixties, calling people "darling" and "sweetie"—like Dickie Attenborough. (Of course it's often because I can't remember their names, but we'll gloss over that.) When I open a door and let someone go first, it's no longer because I feel as if I'm a lowly servantlike person. No, I open the door and let them go first —sometimes actually *insisting* they go first—as a mark of superiority in a power struggle. I'm saying, "I have such ludicrous confidence in myself that it doesn't matter to *me* who goes first!"

Some poet once complained that "the years between fifty and seventy are the hardest. You are always being asked to do things, and you are not yet decrepit enough to turn them down." But I don't find it a problem. I *can* refuse things.

Someone invites me, say, to hear her youngest goddaughter playing the oboe for charity in Ely Cathedral (hundreds of miles away) on a cold January afternoon, and I'm shamelessly able to say, "No, I'm so sorry. It's a bit far. I do wish her the very best. I'd love to give something to the charity, but these days I just can't do oboe concerts in Ely Cathedral. I'm just too bloody *old!*" Well, maybe I put it a bit more politely than that, but that's the basic drift.

It's quite nice, too, now one's older, being able to say quite loopy things like "I'm sorry I can't come to supper—I've got the electrician coming in the following day." It's an excuse that is entirely baffling to the person who's asking you, and is entirely irrefutable.

I've even heard myself say, when someone asks me to go and see a film that doesn't sound very good, "No, I couldn't *possibly* come to that. I know I'll *hate* it." (Oddly, if ever I do have to see it, I find that, increasingly, I'm right in my judgment of films and plays I've never seen.) Age has given me a second sense about movies, rather like that of a blind man who can feel what an object is without seeing it. I only have to read that certain people have given it a good review, certain other people have given it a bad review, watch a trailer on YouTube, and ask certain key friends what they thought of it, and I know at once whether I'm going to like it or not.

Actually, my confidence is such that I know not only whether I'll like it or not but, more crucially, whether it is actually any good or not. Yes, I'm now so old that I no longer say things like "Well, that's your opinion, and this is my opinion." I now know quite categorically not only whether the issue is one that can bear a conclusion like that, or whether it's one about which I have to say, "I will grant you your opinion. But when it comes to judgment, you are wrong. And I am right. There are no two ways about it." (Recently I discovered that Ezra Pound once said, "One of the pleasures of middle age is to find out that one *was* right and that was much righter than one knew at, say, seventeen or twenty-three.")

And, of course, lest anyone think me an old gloombird, I am quite happy these days to go to movies on my own. I don't imagine that if I see someone I know in the foyer they'll see me as a sad old biddy without any friends. I think they'll say to themselves, "She's incredibly bold to go to the cinema on her own. Wish I dared do the same."

Not only that, I'm now confident enough to walk out of films or plays—and not just in the middle or in the intermission. I walk out of them if they don't have the decency to captivate me in the first ten minutes. When you've spent some time watching a lousy movie, little feels more pleasurable, after struggling past dozens of people's knees and making your way blindly up a darkened aisle, than reaching the fresh air and light outside a movie theater and breathing a sigh of relief. Free at last.

It's nice, too, no longer to feel we have to be politically correct. I'm not saying I want to go around talking of golliwogs, because I never did, but the occasional slip, when you're over sixty, is forgivable. And, sometimes, quite useful.

I don't want anyone to get the impression that I've become a member of the "Me" generation. As a baby boomer I was born just at the end of the war, and it's impossible to shake off a feeling that women are put here to serve. And, to be honest, I rather like it. I love taking other people's clothes to the cleaners, doing their shopping and cooking, and making appointments for other people to see the doctor and so on. I actually enjoy trying to make others' lives less stressful and get very miffed if that role is wrenched away from me. I loved being a mum and, during the brief period when it worked, being a wife. It's not because I'm good, but simply because that's how it feels comfortable for me. I'd be hopeless with a whole bunch of servants pandering to my every whim.

But there's no question that it's quite nice, just now and again, having the confidence to say, "No—you go, I don't want to." Or, "Well, if you don't want to, I'll go on my own."

It's My House

I've always had lodgers (see chapter 15, "Alone Again") and they used to terrorize me. Once one of them arrived with a large suitcase. He looked very shifty when I caught him lugging it upstairs. "If anyone asks, you don't know *nothing* about this suitcase," he warned me, in a serious tone. "Nothing, see? And if the fuzz come round, tell 'em I'm out. Even if I'm in. Geddit?"

Another arrived explaining, as I handed her the key, that she'd been kicked out of her last place because of her desire to have candles burning throughout the night. "They chucked me out," she said, wistfully. "The whole place burnt to a crisp. They were livid."

I'd lie in bed imagining they were laughing at me, and, if they had a friend stay over, I would be completely unable to say, "In the future, could you introduce me to anyone I don't know who's coming to stay in my house . . . and first ask my permission, anyway?" I felt like someone in a surreal play, tortured by strange intruders. I hardly dared ask for the rent.

Now I leave crazy Post-it notes on the stairs. "Darling—rent's due. Could I have it by Thursday? And PLEASE keep your radio down before 9 a.m. on Sunday."

The other day, when there was a party going on beyond my garden that was keeping the whole street awake, I simply put on my slippers and dressing gown, marched right around the block, banged on their door, and told them *in no uncertain terms* that I was trying to get some sleep, as were millions of others, and could they at least shut the windows? Even the sight of a couple of teenagers sniggering at me on the stairs didn't faze me.

I've always been very tolerant when it comes to people smoking in my house, allowing them to smoke anywhere, even in the garden. But now if they suggest they smoke in the garden, I simply refuse to let them. "You can perfectly well smoke in the house!" I say, pointing to the various ashtrays lying around. "I'm not having you sneak off and having private chats with other smokers without my being in on the fun. And anyway, I like the smell."

And, final nail in the coffin of shyness, faced with an empty dance floor surrounded by people unable to be the first to start off the rock 'n' rolling (yes, it was one of those middle-aged things) I went up to a complete stranger and asked him to dance.

Restaurants

In the past in restaurants I'd try to hide stuff that I couldn't eat under a cabbage leaf rather than let on to a waiter that what he'd given me was inedible. Stuff that I was *paying* for! These days, however, I can send things back. I'm not horrible. I don't humiliate waiters and demand to see the manager. I just give a great big smile and say, "I'm so sorry, sweetheart, but I think this fish is a tiny bit off." Or sometimes I say, "You couldn't warm this soup up for me, darling? It's a bit on the nippy side." (Of course when they bring it back in a better condition, it's worth confidently saying, "Oh, you're a complete angel, darling, I'm sorry to be such a boring old fusspot"—or something like that. You may laugh and think I sound like a lunatic, but I can assure you, it gets me what I want.)

I think I may well be turning into an Old Bat. Certainly I now have the cunning to precede every call I make to a service industry or complaints bureau or, indeed, almost anyone except my closest friends and relations, with the words, "Hello. I am a retiree. . . ." I'm thinking, when I'm a bit older, to add the words, ". . . and I have cancer," just to make sure I get the attention I deserve.

Strangers

I actually smile at strangers in the street. And I don't mean I'm one of those terrified little old ladies who go around with a permanent smile on their faces . . . my heart always bleeds for them because I imagine they were cruelly treated in their childhood. But sometimes I just dare to smile at someone particularly threatening—and I mean a proper, all-the-way-up-to-the-eyes smile, not a nervous twitch—and though I don't often get a smile back, it's certainly worth it when I do. I've even been known to smile at hoodlums. "Hello, darling!" I don't actually say to them, but I'm thinking it. "Hello, you *angel!* I'm an old lady and I can smile at you because I am no threat to you whatsoever!"

They Don't Scare Me Anymore

The confidence comes, you see, not with just not feeling others are a threat, but actually no longer *being* a threat. And if I'm not frightened of you and you're not frightened of me, then that breeds confidence—and friendliness—on both sides. When I was young, everyone older than me was frightening. Forty-year-olds were frightening. Now they're just like big kids.

When I was young I used to dread going to the hospital because I always felt so powerless. But the last time I was in, I got the hang of it. I refused to be called Virginia—and once the nurses start calling you by your last name (in my case Ms. Ironside) they automatically, if involuntarily, show a great deal more respect.

I scored two victories last time I was in. A nurse who looked as old as my mother (but who, I had to remind myself, was probably *younger* than me), tried to insist I wore slippers to walk down the corridor. I simply laughed and said, "I don't wear slippers." She insisted and I repeated, "I don't think you heard, my dear. I *don't wear slippers!*" Collapse of stout party.

Next they tried to force me into a pair of hot white stockings in the middle of summer to stop me getting an embolism (I think). "Darlings," I said, grandly, "if I wanted to look like an understudy from *Pagliacci*, I would have painted my face white and brought a red nose with me into the hospital. I am too *old* for fun and games like that." As none of the poor mites had any idea of what I was talking about, the white stockings were quickly bundled out of the way.

Public Speaking

The prospect of reciting "To Autumn" by Keats at a school concert when I was young reduced me to a gibbering wreck. My palms sweated, my legs trembled, my heart thundered and I felt sick. Now—I can hardly bear to admit this—if anyone asks who would like to deliver a eulogy at a funeral, I feel my hand shooting up before they've even got the words out. I am doing a one-woman show at Edinburgh. How on earth has this come about? It's not just because I love public speaking. It's also because of experience. Forced into talking to ladies' luncheon clubs by an editor when I worked on a women's magazine in the '70s, I now realize that I can talk to a bunch of old ladies who are all snoring their heads off and the world doesn't come to an end. Having done a book tour, I know that if one person—a very crazy and probably homeless person at that—is the only member of the audience, I can still stagger my way through a script. And if it's bad, and I get just a sad handful of applause—for which I'm lucky because I've often had to face the sound of the scraping of chairs as people left all the way through the performance—it simply doesn't matter all that much. I merely try to tell myself, as I experience the shame and disappointment, that "This, too, will pass." And because I'm older, I know that it will. (It's odd—the confidence of age doesn't seem to apply to driving or traveling, about which on the whole older people get more frightened rather than more confident. But perhaps that's because they know too many of the possible pitfalls; see the Anxiety section in "Ailments.")

It's no good telling a young person that. How are they to know you're right? But when you're older you know that nothing lasts, neither happiness nor misery. And that knowledge makes you a whole lot braver.

Where Does the Bravado Come From?

We're braver, partly, because we don't fear death so much. We know it's got to come sooner or later, so there's much more point in living for the moment. Which leads on to the feeling that there's not much time left. At sixty-five you'd be lucky to have twenty years left of life, and it's silly spending any of those twenty years sitting through crap films or talking to people you don't like or doing things you don't want to do. I don't mean that one should forgo the duties that society imposes on us and be totally irresponsible, but perhaps we needn't feel quite as beholden as we used to. We've spent our lives doing things for other people. It's our turn to have a few people, just sometimes, do things for us.

The Confidence to Ask for Help

When I was young I did everything for myself. I changed my own tires, I painted my own ceilings, I repaired my own furniture, and I made my own picture frames. I recaned the seats of chairs and wired up new lamps. I grew my plants from seed and I even, once, rehung my own front door, having shaved a bit off the bottom to make it fit. That's what we did in the '60s and '70s, partly to show that we were as good as men at doing practical things but partly, in my case at least, because it was tremendous fun. I once made an entire Ping-Pong table for the family. Hung my own wallpaper. The only things I drew the line at were cleaning my own chimneys, carpeting my own floors, and felling my own trees.

Now? Well, let's be honest. It would not be impossible for me to do any of those things. But the great thing about being old is that you don't *have* to. And, when you don't do these things, you don't lose any face. I would have felt like a bit of an idiot if, when I was thirty, I was found standing on a roadside begging for help from a man because I'd gotten a flat tire. I'd have been horrified if a man asked, politely, if he could carry my suitcase up the steps at a railway station. I would have cringed if I'd used a free disabled toilet without being disabled. But now, as an older woman, I don't feel I lose any dignity at all when I ask for help. If there's anything that needs doing that requires a bit more effort than I can be bothered to make, my mantra now is "I'll get a man in."

Of course, in an emergency, I'd be out there with my Black & Decker, no worries. If battling grannies can ward off robbers by wielding mops (and every day one reads of these resourceful creatures who repel drug-crazed robbers simply by making ghastly faces at them and boxing their ears), I could, if I wanted to, build my own shelves. But I just don't *want* to any more.

We sixty-year-olds are part of a blessed generation. When we were young we were idolized, as young people—because young people had only just been discovered. In Britain we have had free education, and a pretty good health service.

We've never directly experienced a war. Even now, however lame or crippled we may be, we feel ourselves to be in some way special—we're not, of course, and we know it intellectually, but since we've always been treated as new, fresh, and interesting, unsurprisingly, for lots of us, that feeling has stuck.

We are, in our sixties at least (and don't let's think about some of the horrors that may await us), caught in the wonderful interface between youth and ancientness. The old French saying runs *"Si jeunesse savait, si vieillesse pouvait"* —which means "If the young only knew, if the old only could." But in our sixties we actually have the chance to both know *and* be able.

Bliss.

4. Spare Time

If you want to get a favor done
    by some obliging friend,
And want a promise, safe and sure,
    on which you may depend,
Don't go to him who always has
    much leisure time to plan,
If you want your favor done,
    just ask the busy man.

The man with leisure never has
    a moment he can spare,
He's always "putting off" until
    his friends are in despair.
But he whose every waking hour
    is crowded full of work
Forgets the art of wasting time,
    he cannot stop to shirk.

So when you want a favor done,
    and want it right away,
Go to the man who constantly
    works twenty hours a day
He'll find a moment somewhere,
    that has no other use
And help you, while the idle man
    is framing an excuse.

—Anonymous

"THE PROBLEM WITH RETIRED PEOPLE," said a young friend of mine the other day, "is that they're so incredibly *busy*."

When you retire, you often wonder what on earth you're going to be doing with all the time you've got. But all I can advise you to do is to make the most of those few short days that you have, after retirement, when you feel just a teensy bit bored.

Parkinson's Law is: "Work expands so as to fill the time available for its completion." Well, his law applies just as well to leisure.

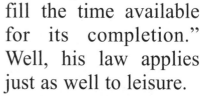

After you've given Saturday over to the grandchildren, Sunday over to having people to lunch, and Monday for the reading for the Book Club (if you belong to one, of course; I have other interests, such as ballroom dancing), then Tuesday writing all those complaining letters on behalf of the Residents' Association, and Wednesday doing a stint of volunteer reading at the local school, followed by Thursday— Genealogy Day—and Friday catching up on cooking, cleaning, shopping, phoning, e-mailing, and generally staring at the computer for hours on end—there's not much time in between except for the odd snooze. And as for the gardening . . . and the charity work . . . God knows when there'll be time for those.

Here are some suggestions—and pros and cons—for those who find, after retirement, that they are at a loose end.

Get a New Life

It's quite tempting, isn't it? Reinvent yourself? It's true, you could place yourself in an artificial environment, like a plant, and try to produce one last fruit even though it's the middle of your winter. These late bloomers tend to veer away from their old careers and do what they say they really wanted to do all along if only they'd had the time. Often this involves things like learning about life in the court of Louis XIV or the intricacies of the women's suffrage movement. They're happy slaving away over hot essays with a malted milk by their side, and some even go away for the odd week to attend seminars and lectures.

Frankly, the very idea of starting up learning again makes my heart sink. First of all, being a writer, the idea of writing an essay for *nothing* seems to me to make no sense whatsoever. I'm so used to writing for a living that I can barely dash off a thank-you letter without attaching an invoice. Second, surely, I did all that essay writing when I was young? Could I really bear to sit chewing my pencil, trying to eke out another two hundred words about the development, say, of public health in Bedfordshire between 1858 and 1859—and then hand it in to some twelve-year-old chit of a professor who has the power, not to mention temerity, actually to *mark my stuff?*

I thought I'd said good-bye to the university refectory, the grimness of a locker, and the sheer terror inspired by a library.

The other problem about getting a new life is that learning a new skill just isn't that easy when you're old. The best time to learn things is probably when you're about seven . . . but when you're just about to turn seventy the old brain cells aren't working with such agility as they used to. The synapses are shriveling, and our mental pathways have already gotten worn, like old cart tracks. The soil of our brain is no longer soft and malleable, but needs a great deal of drilling and hacking to penetrate.

You can, of course, take up something you've never tried in your life, and use bits of your brain previously untouched by human thought, such as learning to become a blues pianist or trying to replicate the craft of Chinese pottery making in the nineteenth century. But rather than become a mediocre watercolorist at sixty-five, wouldn't it be better to build on something you already know something about, and are familiar with? Look at subjects in which you already have a grounding and work on them. Were you an expert dressmaker when you were young? Could you now go back to it or branch out into upholstering, a skill along the same lines—rather than try to learn how to draw from scratch, a near-impossible task when you're ancient?

The problem with getting a new life, if that's your aim, is that so often you die halfway through it. I've had countless friends move to Italy to convert an old farmhouse and then— bingo, just as they're about to put the final tile on the new roof, one of them pops off, leaving the other with the ghastly burden of a vast Italian estate and no one to share it with.

Don't Get a New Life

One reason I'm so against getting a new life is that I've been trying most of my life to get a new life, and I'll tell you why I'm so pleased now to stick with the one I've got. When I was young, a woman's aim was never much more than to get a secretarial job and then marry and have children. I knew I didn't want a career, I had a Career Mum and I didn't like it.

It's true that when I was about ten, I harbored vague ambitions of becoming a world-famous opera singer (emphasis, of course, on the "world-famous"). Musically, I was reasonably good at the piano, though I certainly didn't excel at it. But then my father gave me a 78 rpm record (a big old heavy vinyl disc) of Lily Pons singing Delibes's "Bell Song" from *Lakmé*—a staggering piece of coloratura. And I found that, after a bit of practice, I got the hang of coloratura singing. My pitch has always been pretty good. And I absolutely loved singing along with Lily.

Then there was the duet from *La Traviata* and soon I found that I could sing along with both parts, man and woman, pretty spot-on. I realized that I had a rather good range. And although I never asked for singing lessons, I secretly longed for years to be an opera singer. (About ten years ago, when I was fifty-five, I did have a singing lesson and have to say I was rather crushed when the young girl teaching me, clearly clueless, didn't seem to be remotely impressed by my voice.)

All through my life I'd had yearnings to be things other than a writer or journalist. When I was twenty-eight, I longed to be an academic of some sort. I applied to college, but halfway through the second term I cracked up completely, was carried out of the library by men in white coats, and was put into a nursing home in Primrose Hill. Then I got it into my head that I'd like to be a teacher. I signed up for the course, and dreamed of giving up journalism and running a school, as my great-aunt had done in the '40s. But after ten days, I dropped out.

About five years ago, when I was sixty, I found I was *still* wondering what I would do when I grew up. Obviously, when people asked me what I did I answered that I was a journalist or advice columnist or writer, but I never really believed it. Suddenly I looked back on my life and realized that over the years I had written millions upon millions of words. I had had, in my time, produced more than a dozen columns in magazines and newspapers, and written more than fifteen books. Could it be that all this time, while I was dreaming of another career, I *was* actually a writer, all along? A real one? Not just someone pretending to be a writer?

It is only now that all those other career options have finally dropped away. As I feel the burden of guilt for not following those paths roll away from my shoulders, I experience an incredible sense of relief. I know who I am. Or, rather, what I am. At last. I'm not going to start changing anything now. Coming to terms with one's present life is, I promise you, far more fulfilling than starting off a new one.

Take a First-Aid Course

You may wonder what might be the point of this, but remember that as we get older and older we also get sicker and sicker and it would be nice, when your companion suffers a seizure, or is suddenly unable to heave himself from the bath, or chokes on a fishbone, or complains of her left arm becoming paralyzed, to be able to leap into action and save your companion from certain death. Who knows, you might actually be lucky enough to be around when someone experiences "the Drop" (see "Ailments") and wouldn't you be the hero if you knew all about the recovery position and could perform a tracheotomy with a humble ballpoint pen?

SKIing

SKIers are those people who spend their old age Spending the Kids' Inheritance. Oh, it's all very good fun, isn't it, the idea of squandering all your wealth so your kids can't get their hands on it, but—excuse me while I purse my lips into a narrow line of disapproval and get serious—I really don't think it's right. The welcome thud of a dollop of cash going into your bank account when a parent dies certainly takes some of the edge off the loss—though I suppose if you had the sort of people who are SKIers as parents, you wouldn't feel a hell of a lot of loss anyway. Myself, I wouldn't advise this course of action. I would prefer to *Save* for my Kids' Inheritance, and fantasize about them in the future setting up vast empires based on the humble sum that I have managed to scrape together to leave them in my will. But then I just can't help being nice, responsible, and noble. Sickening, isn't it?

Dive into the Past

If I so much as started to try to sort all my old photographs into albums, it would take me at least a year. (And oh dear, I just haven't got time, *you* know. What with the charities, the Residents' Association, the gym . . .) But some old people absolutely love getting their histories in order.

And researching the family tree can use up an inordinate amount of time. I have friends who are so taken up with discovering that their old relatives were knife-grinders in the fifteenth century, or butlers in the sixteenth, that they slave away even on weekends to discover ancestors who, to be honest, often sound just as boring as they are.

Recently a friend of mine called me and asked if she could pop over because she had something really interesting to tell me. I welcomed her over, made her a cup of coffee, chatted of this and that, and then leaned forward, all ears, to hear the latest tasty bit of gossip.

"Well," she said. "You'll never believe this, but I've just been down to the Family Records Office and I discovered that my great-great-grandmother lived in a small village in Lincolnshire and took in dressmaking!"

I have to say that the old jaw didn't exactly

drop. And what would the correct reaction be to that extraordinarily uninspiring piece of news, anyway? Sometimes an old relative will take me for a tour of the family tree and we leap from branch to branch with him (it's usually a him) explaining marriages in 1548 while I try to pinch myself awake.

The other day a relative I'd never met traveled all the way from Edinburgh to see me and have a cup of tea, armed with charts, trees, marriage and death certificates, and all kinds of paperwork that he wanted to share with me. I thought I would die of boredom. But then all he would have done is just note the date of my death and add it to his wretched tree.

Just because I don't have the same enthusiasm for ancestry that some people have, however, doesn't mean I should knock it. It may well be your thing and if so, good luck to you. After all, there is an old Chinese proverb that goes: "To forget your ancestors is to be a brook without a source, a tree without a root." But what do they know?

Graveyards these days are simply heaving with couples with clipboards, searching for the remains of their old rellies, and when I have, on occasion, been forced into the Family Records Office in London, I've marveled at the sight of row upon row of oldies, all in Windbreakers, staring at computers (the man is usually the one with his hand on the mouse; the wife is usually squinting at the screen as he scrolls through pages and pages of old relatives). The scene in the FRO is reminiscent of a Moonie mass marriage. Or a rally in North Korea. Or some vision summoned up by a kaleidoscope, a never-ending vista of oldies staring into their pasts.

If you've already found out who all your ancestors are from Year One, then don't despair. You can start on your house. I have found out, by consulting the 1911 census, that my house used to be lived in by two waiters and their wives, and a dressmaker who was married to a steward, with a couple of children. Not sure quite where it gets me but it is, briefly, interesting. (What is particularly odd, it struck me, is that my house doesn't actually *belong* to me. It is an illusion. It is actually something I lease only for my lifetime, as it were. When they were living here, the dressmakers and stewards thought it was *their* house, and when I'm dead someone else will imagine it is *their* house. I felt rather irrationally cross with my house after this discovery, like I imagine it would feel if you found —and read—dozens of love letters written to your husband before you married him.)

Look over Old Amstrad Disks
Recently I was asked to update a book I'd written around fifteen years ago. Unfortunately I'd written it on an old Amstrad, a computer that

dates back to the time before computers were invented, which had long been chucked on the trash heap. Struck by a wild hope, I wondered if by any chance I'd kept the old Amstrad disks I'd written the book on originally. And there, in a dusty pile under the long-out-of-date prescription goggles and some shriveled diving flippers, I found in an old plastic box a three-inch disk: a copy of the entire book.

How I blessed myself for not throwing it away! But how could I retrieve the information? How could I get it to yield up its secrets? It was only a matter of moments before, on the Internet, I found an amazing company, a one-man outfit in Cornwall whose motto was "Clinging to the trailing edge of technology" and promised, for a mere five dollars, the transfer of all my old information onto a sparkling new state-of-the-art Microsoft Word disk.

Talking to the man who ran it was like entering a lost world. We discussed LocoScript, CP/M disks (the ones no one ever used because that turned the whole thing into a computer and we didn't want any of that monkey business), ASCII files, and the dreaded Limbo. We reminisced about the Start of Day disk and the "daisy wheel" printer. I told him of the time, before I turned into the granorak I am today, that my son insisted I get an Amstrad and wrestle with new technology.

And he told me his strange life in the land of Amstrad—the veritable Morris Minor of the computer world.

It's incredible to think that some people are still using them. Like finding there are still airship services to Le Touquet, daily. Okay, the assistants at the computer store may look at you goggle-eyed if you mention the word, but there are still users in the outback of Australia, there are one or two in the United States, and (tellingly) a large concentration around Norwich, a cluster in Cumbria, and quite a few in the northeast of Scotland up toward Cromarty. And who are these strange users? They are ministers of religion who, desperate for ideas, need to sort through the archives for something to serve up, reheated, on a Sunday; they are novelists and poets. Some elderly people want to retrieve information on LocoScript files because they're writing down memories for their families, and some younger people, after a parent has died, want to discover what the hell their mums or dads got up to on their old computers.

The discovery of those disks really says something for hoarding. Indeed, sometimes, swamped by spam and pop-up windows, I even wish I'd still kept the loyal old Amstrad itself.

I'm waiting for the day when I have time actually to trawl through all my old disks, file by file. To rediscover your past self: Wouldn't that be a whole lot more interesting than finding out about other people?

Which brings me to . . .

Write Your Life Story

They do say that everyone has at least one book in them, so where's yours? Writing your life story is a wonderful activity that includes *everything* I've mentioned so far—family research, old Amstrad disks, sorting out piles of old photographs, and even talking to contemporaries you'd forgotten all about. It's not dry, like genealogy; you can try your hand at fine writing if you wish, and you can not only give bouquets and leave tributes at the feet of all those exceptional people you've known all your life, but also get revenge on boorish schoolteachers or bosses. You could even design your own cover.

Added to this, you have all the fun of self-publishing (sorry, don't kid yourself that any publisher except one you pay will be remotely interested in your life unless you have had a hundred boob jobs, discovered you are the secret love child of Elvis Presley, been on a reality TV show, or murdered several prostitutes in your time). Presto! All your Christmas-present problems solved in one fell swoop.

And channeling all your energy into writing your life story will prevent you from boring your grandchildren sick as you tell them about What

It Was Like Just After the War (see "Boring for Britain").

Leave Your Partner

Oh, I *know,* I shouldn't even suggest this, should I? But it could be your very last chance for happiness. Particularly if you've found a gorgeous younger model. Even if you haven't got a young stud or studette waiting in the wings, you can read the chapter "Alone Again" and find out the advantages—and disadvantages—of being single.

Reexamine Old Hates

When I was young I had a complete prejudice about three things. If anyone said that they admired mime or puppetry or Marcel Proust, I would go to my address book and cross out their names with a black felt-tipped pen. Those areas all spelled, for me, the last word in pretension.

Age has changed me. Nowadays I'd far rather go to see mime than a play, puppets score higher than American movies, and as for Proust— well, have you actually *read* him? He is totally wonderful! He'll take up a good year of your life, anyway. Recommend him to your Book Club and that'll shut them up for a while.

It's surprising how many childhood prejudices can turn into huge pleasures when you're older. Not just sprouts.

Knitting

There is a fashion for sneering at knitting. I heard an interview with the author of a knitting book on the radio last year and the way the presenter patronized her completely enraged me. "But you could be . . ." she exclaimed, flailing around in her effort to think of things that would be better to do than knitting. "You could be *going to the gym!*" "Or," chimed in a smarmy guest, "you could be *reading a book!*"

Can you think of anything less productive, more self-indulgent, or time wasting than reading a book or going to the gym? This knitter was producing, over the months, sweaters, socks, hats—she'd even knitted an apron—blankets, vests . . . while what would the gym-goers and readers have to show for their efforts? Precisely nothing. I have to say I rather sympathize, when people go on about the marvels of reading, with my grandmother's mother who used to fly into a rage when she found my grandmother curled up in a corner with a book. "Reading a book!" she'd splutter, furiously. "Why aren't you out there, *doing something!*"

The roasting that this wretched knitter got from the two liberal feminist ladies on the radio galvanized me into racing up to the department store, finding a knitting pattern, wool, and needles, and sitting down immediately to get clicking. I knitted some tiny socks for my grandson—on four needles, no less—a hat, and my current project is a sweater. Knitting is one of the most soothing, creative, meditative, and useful ways of occupying yourself in the whole world. You can even listen to the radio—and fume—while you do it.

Exercise

My exercise routine involves getting out of bed, going downstairs, having a bath, going upstairs to sit at a computer, going downstairs for a cup of coffee, and *occasionally* walking to my car. But lots of old people I know actually spend a couple of hours a week at the gym.

The last time I went to a gym the air was thick with the smell of testosterone. My eyes were blinded by the light glancing off well-oiled biceps and the noise (of some kind of music that I wouldn't dream of trying to identify) was deafening. Since I can barely lift anything heavier than a pencil, I felt utterly ashamed to be unable to lift the appropriate weight, and if I'm going to gasp and sweat I'd prefer to do it in the privacy of my own home rather than in front of row upon row of lissom young bodies. Going to the gym undoubtedly made me fitter physically, but mentally I felt like a crushed worm as I crawled home to jump into a bath to wash off all the gymmy smell. As for swimming . . . as W. C. Fields said, about water, "Fish fuck in it." Who knows who uses my local pool as a lavatory, but since even I have, on occasion, when much younger, relieved myself slightly in a pool when desperate, I can't believe that others haven't been known, just occasionally, to do the same.

The other thing is that it's so *boring*. As a woman, I like to do two—or sometimes three— things at once. I couldn't possibly sit down to listen to a radio play, for instance. I have to be ironing or knitting (see above), or fixing something at the same time. Gardening is a much more productive way to take exercise if you're lucky enough to own a patch of earth behind your home, or even walking to the local store—at least there's a goal. And isn't it funny how I'm able to lug back a couple of shopping bags stuffed with two-liter plastic cartons of milk, three boxes of orange juice, two sacks of potatoes, and a couple of gigantic melons with comparative ease, while a couple of tiny weights at the gym leave me frazzled.

Another favorite exercise routine for old people is the "aquagym." The reasoning behind this, I gather, is that because of the pressure of water, you exercise your muscles really well without actually having to do anything weight-bearing, which might put pressure on your crumbling old bones. But the sight of a group of old ladies trying to walk across the width of a swimming pool like spacemen is so appalling that I've tried it only once. There is a limit to the humiliation one can suffer when one's old. And aquagym is my own personal limit. Luckily, I am now confident enough (see "Confidence") to say no to aquagym ever again.

Having said all this to put you off, I know some people do actually enjoy going to the gym, and come out feeling energized and ready for anything. Exercise is said to relieve depression. I just haven't got the time or the desire.

New Gadgetry

If, like me, you have a phobia about new gadgetry, then resolve, if you have nothing better to do, to overcome it. I'm speaking here as someone who, when my son unveiled the mysteries of the new Amstrad to me, burst into floods of tears, had to be restrained from throwing the whole machine out of the window, and spent the rest of the week unable to go into my workroom for terror of the thing.

So if it's possible for me to make a friend of LocoScript (and, later, to become reconciled to his younger brother, Windows), then it's possible for you to become a granorak and go and get a new cell phone with a camera in it, become accomplished at redesigning your snaps on Photoshop, hurl yourself into the mysteries of a BlackBerry, learn how to configure a new flat-screen television (recording, no less, onto the hard drive of your DVR), and download all your old VHS tapes onto DVDs. I'm not saying I can do all these things. But if I had time, I would certainly hire a man (a young man, in this case) and force him to explain it to me step by step.

The Crossword Puzzle

Now, I won't have anyone knocking the crossword puzzle. I've loved it ever since, as a child, I used to do it with my grandmother in the evening. Those were the days when the clues featured quotes from poetry with blanks in them, like "Season of _____ and mellow fruitfulness" (Keats) 5, and I would look them up in her *Oxford Book of Quotations*. "Mists!" she'd repeat, when I told her the answer. "How very useful. That gives us a very useful *m* in 7 down and a rather interesting *s* in 10 across. How clever you are, darling. What *would* I do without you?"

I always remember my grandfather telling me his favorite clue was "Napier's admission of wrongdoing in India." The answer was (as any fool knows, when he recalls that General Napier took the town of Sind in India and had to convey the news to his superiors in a telegram without anyone finding out) Peccavi.* Oh I know that this will baffle the non-crossword-doers

_____
* I have sinned

94

among you, but the sheer genius of that clue and the answer delight me still today. (My own favorite is "Bottle party? Impossible!" [2,3,2].[*])

These days I do the Jumbo cryptic in the London *Times* with a friend who lives in the Lake District. We do it together on the telephone, and great fun it is, too. Not only is it meant to keep the brain lively (though I'm not sure how true this is), it gives one a great excuse for hauling out reference books—you can spend a lot of the last years of your life looking up the derivation of words in the dictionary—and boring each other to bits with information like "Yes, an *oilee* was indeed a young miner in the Welsh pits—and *oilie* is someone who has done very well out of oil, according to up-to-date New York slang. So, if it says 'sounds like,' it must be *oilee*." "Or *oilie*," says my friend from the Lakes dejectedly. "They both fit. We'll never know which is right."

Give Up

You can do what you like. Get up when you want. Sleep when you want. Watch movies in the afternoon. Eat when you like. Go where you like, when you like.

But there is a lot to be said for winding down and spending the rest of your life pottering about in your slippers, peering at Google every

[*] No can do

day, and filling the hours between dawn and dusk answering thorny questions like, "Should I have another cup of tea now or later?"

One friend of mine told me, "It's so great now, being able simply to loaf around. I don't think I've done any proper loafing since I was fourteen."

While lots of oldies see the decade or so that follows sixty as an opening to a new, adventurous world, for me it's not the sound of doors opening that I love. It's the slamming sound of doors shutting that I like, making space for much more parochial pleasures.

Birds and Gardening

If you're anything like me, you'll find, after sixty, you turn more inward than outward. I'm far fussier about my house than I used to be, and having always thought birds rather a waste of airspace, I have now become obsessed with the blackbirds, robins, and so on in my garden. I have actually bought that very thing that I used to dread my grandmother bringing out, a Bird Book, which tells you whether you have a lesser spotted nuthatch on your doorstep or a greater crested wagtail. I even have a bird feeder, and a cat-scarer, and subscribe to a site that tells me Which Kinds of Nuts Attract Which Kinds of Bird. Unfortunately, of course, due to my ripening cataracts, I am unable to tell the difference between all the brown things that come hopping about my garden, but I like to think the lawn is awash with goldfinches, tits, and chaffinches.

Then, of course, there's gardening, something I used to regard with dread as a kind of outdoor housework. They do say that gardening is an elderly way of satisfying some kind of parental instinct, that we always want to nurture and grow things. It's just in our nature. The kids have fled the nest, so we've got to make do with nasturtiums instead. (The great things about nasturtiums, you will find if you grow enough of them, is that they never fly the nest. They just reseed, meaning, when they die, you never have to spend hours in the bedroom sobbing your eyes out and then, when you get up, pretending that you don't mind at all.)

I try to grow things from seed, and very pleased I am when one in about a hundred actually makes it to the flowering stage.

But beware. Recently I read that apparently, according to scientists, thirty minutes of digging, weeding, and pruning five times a week can revitalize sexual performance. Such moderate exercise is enough to reduce the risk of impotence by around 38 percent. So don't go mad. Unless, of course, you want more sex. Which means you haven't yet read the chapter on sex.

5. Death

There is one great thing about dying, which is that you don't have to get out of bed to do it.

—Kingsley Amis

A S AN AGONY AUNT, I try to understand most things. I can understand people harming themselves, I can understand their being phobic about signing their names in public, I can imagine that some might find pleasure in any number of strange sexual practices. But I've always had a bit of a blind spot when it comes to people who are frightened of death. It might be, of course, that I've so often thought about it. Even when I was in my twenties, I decided very firmly that if life didn't improve by the time I was thirty, I would jump off a cliff. It

PAST
SELL-BY
DATE

didn't improve but by then I had a son, and therefore the cliff jumping had to wait, and so it continued, until now, when I'm left with fewer (I hope) years ahead of me than years behind me—and I'm starting to think there isn't much point in cliff jumping when it's going to happen so soon anyway. It's rather like reading a book at bedtime. It may be two in the morning and you're dying to go to sleep but when you see you've only got twenty pages left, you stagger on till you reach the end rather than leaving it unread till the next day.

I see death as something rather wonderful to look forward to. I see it like coming home. I see it as a merciful relief from all life's anxieties and troubles. I see it as a longed-for respite—and the idea of coming back again, even as a chirpy robin, let alone a human being, fills me with horror. The other thing is, of course, that it's going to happen to *all of us*. So why not welcome it and accept it rather than dread it? Everyone around me always goes on about how stupid people are who see life as a glass half empty rather than a glass half full, so why can't they feel the same optimistic way about death? It would seem sensible. When older people call up and say, tearfully, "Oh no, I've been told I've only got a few months to live," I tend to think, Well, what do you expect at your age, dearie? I don't imagine you were expecting to live forever.

As a seventy-five-year-old friend said to me the other day, having just come away from a grisly candlelit vigil beside an eighty-five-year-old friend who had suffered from Parkinson's disease hideously for ten years and had been dying of it for the last ten days, "Why all this surprise over death? After all, you and I don't have a special relationship with it. All the signs that we're going to die have been there from the very day we were born."

Us oldies have had years and years to get used to the idea of death. We shouldn't be so pathetic about it, we shouldn't dread it. We should set a good example to the young, and teach them, too, to welcome death, when life gets too wretched, or when it's clear that we've spent quite enough time at the party and our hosts are starting to yawn and look at the clock.

It's a Great Time to Die, Anyway

That's another plus for us oldies. The recession is settling in for a couple of decades, global warming (if you believe it, that is) spells the end of the earth as we know it, and, frankly, there's not a lot of fascinating stuff looming on the horizon. It would have been horrible to have died during, say, the Renaissance. You'd be kicking yourself for not being around to see the glorious works of art, and read about the amazing scientific discoveries and new theories that you knew must be in the air. But now, at the risk of sounding like an old bore (see "Boring for Britain") what *is* there to look forward to? Literature has pretty much reached a dead end, books themselves appear to be a dying art, and soon we're going to have to read everything on screens, which is literally a pain in the neck; modern classical music is well-nigh incomprehensible; the last art exhibition I went to sent me home reeling. The world is being taken over by machines, you can't even talk to an operator on the telephone anymore, and we are all gradually going to become less and less individualized and more like one another. The last time I felt a frisson of real excitement about what was going on around me was in the '60s, and I don't think the jaded feeling I have at the moment about the state of the arts and civilization is entirely because I am ancient. There is a hint of the end of this civilization in the air, a fin de siècle zeitgeist, and I certainly am quite excited about being part of the *fin*.

Isn't Death Fascinating?

I've seen a number of people dying and they all went off, at the very end, incredibly peacefully, so there's nothing to fear. Many were pleased. Even Freud said, in a letter he wrote to a friend in 1936, "I still cannot get used to the grief and afflictions of old age and I look forward with longing to the journey into the void."

None of those I saw die shook their fists at close of day, or raged—raged "against the dying of the light," as Dylan Thomas suggested. Indeed, the last words of three of them were impeccably polite. They said "thank you" for some small kindness; then they closed their eyes and died. And a young relation of mine actually said a day before his death, "You know, Virginia, every day a bit of my body shuts down —I can't stand up anymore, or I can't lift a cup to my lips—and it's so odd but I don't mind. I can't tell you how incredibly *interesting* it all is."

That's the spirit.

And What's So Great about Living, Anyway?

The problem is that so many people see living long as some kind of competition. When the author and playwright Simon Gray was told he had only a year to live, he realized his vocabulary about death was slanted. He referred to himself or other people as having "made it to" or "got to" a certain age—and when thinking of someone who died, he reminisced that had he lived he would have "pulled off" another fifteen years.

They say that old age isn't too bad when you consider the alternative. But what is the alternative? Everlasting life? No thanks.

Nowhere is the desire to live long seen so

clearly as in Miami, a city also known as God's Waiting Room. It's rather like Hove, with gangsters. When I was there recently, I descended in an elevator from my hotel room, about five billion floors up; when I got to the three-billionth floor, the door opened to welcome a very elderly, very clean old man, wearing a spotless linen suit and sporting a silver-topped cane. He had that creamy white hair in which you can see every comb line. No egg stain on his tie. The thought almost flitted through my mind that I might quite like to have his grandchildren. There was a silence and then, as we crawled down the remaining floors, he suddenly turned to me with a look of pride and said, in a gravelly voice, "I'm ninety-eight years old."

Now, I expect one of my grandsons to tell me proudly that he is four and a half, but I don't expect a mature person to announce their age. Perhaps this poor guy does nothing all day except *be ninety-eight*. And anyway, what was I to say? "Oh, very good"? Or, more honestly, "Poor you! I do hope life doesn't go on too long. It'll all end soon, I promise."

I find this curious pride in old age all over the place. Even the man who helps out at my local mosque pulls me toward him and whispers in my ear, "I'm eighty-nine." But at least he has the sense and decency to add, rather sadly, "Old age is not merciful."

Certainly everyone in Miami looked fantastically old. You see alarmingly pulled-back face-lifty faces atop crinkled bent old figures, all out of kilter. You imagine that when they're 150 they'll be trying to persuade each other that it's the "new 130."

In America I gave talks to groups of people who all looked just like a sea of wrinkles, ancient specimens, most of whom were apparently held together by pieces of string. Could it have been that they may have had what, in my hotel spa, was advertised as a "longevity massage"—and if so, what did it involve? For some reason I imagined bodies being stretched out as on a rack. In the lobby there was a book for sale called *Secrets of Longevity: 100 Tips on How to Live to 100*. Heaven preserve me. What I wanted was a book called *How to Make Sure You've Popped off by 75: 100 Tips for a Quick and Painless Death*.

To be fair, most people I know do say they're not frightened of death so much as frightened of *dying*. And none of us wants to enter a strange half-life of pain, blindness, deafness, the loss of all our faculties, and, often, a complete change of personality. Some Alzheimer's sufferers can actually turn violent and assault those they previously loved. That is no life for *anyone*.

I have seen a friend die recently, on a life-support machine, her body covered with tubes, wires, with no hope at all of recovery, surrounded by people arguing for days over whether they should choose an option known, apparently, as Power Off. Thank God the sensible people prevailed and she was put out of her misery.

What people are put through these days when it comes to death is worse than it is for animals —not that animals have a great time. When I had a dying cat, I took him to the vet to be put to sleep, but in this new, extraordinary climate of "right to live," even the vet was reluctant. The poor animal had to live on in great pain for three weeks before he almost expired on a Sunday night, and the emergency vet told me that I had a "very big decision to make." "I've made it!" I screamed. "Put him out of his misery now!"

So when some argue about keeping people alive, come what may, I feel like saying, "For heaven's sake, what's the big deal?" I've already lived far longer than most people were expected to live a hundred years ago. At sixty-five, I feel I live on borrowed time and every day's a bonus. As Proust wrote, "We are all dead people, waiting to take up our posts."

Anyway, isn't there a moment when even the most life-loving among us feel we've just had enough? I'm sixty-five and the prospect of another ten Christmases stretching out in front of me, with all the agonies of "are they going to spend it with me, am I going to them, are they going away to their friends?" fills me with dread. Not to mention the fact that it's not good for our children if we hang around too long. I certainly didn't even begin to feel like a grown-up until both my parents had popped off.

Free up Some Space

I know that when your last parent dies you can feel lost. Finally you're an orphan. But you are, at last, free. My own parents seemed like a couple of vast rhododendron bushes hanging over me, for most of my life. When they died, I missed them—but at last I, too, could see the sky and get the warmth of the sun. At last I could grow myself. And I often give thanks to my parents for having had the consideration to die when I was still young enough to enjoy a life free of their affectionate but sometimes stifling presence.

I have friends of seventy-five who are still looking after a bonkers old parent, still staggering off to the nursing home to sit by the bedside of a wheezing half corpse that doesn't even recognize them, and then staggering home again. I have friends whose lives are dominated by their elderly parents. It's not right that older people should hang around, clogging up the corridors, like guests at a party who'll never leave. How will young people ever have a chance to develop if they're forever shadowed by our ailing, brooding presences?

We're living far too long as it is, anyway. By 2040 the number of people over the age of sixty-four is expected to grow from 9.5 million to 15 million. Scientists predict that someone born at the end of this century could expect to live twenty years longer than their equivalent a hundred years before. It's a ghastly prospect. Indeed, Martin Amis has talked of a future in which there is a virtual war between the old and the young, with the old clogging up the hospitals and monopolizing the social services. He spoke recently about a "silver tsunami" overwhelming the younger generation and causing major civil unrest.

Being Bumped Off

Baroness Warnock said that she would far rather die than be put into a nursing home and spend large sums of money that could be better used by her children. My thoughts exactly. And if you think I'm being creepy, apparently 80 percent of us welcome the idea of assisted suicide when we get too old, confused, or ill to enjoy life any more.

I have a living will stashed in almost every room in my house, in my wallet, with my doctor, with my lawyer. My poor son has been told so many times how much I want him to get rid of me if I become a burden, I'm sometimes surprised he doesn't just seize a cushion and do it now, just to shut me up.

Bumping Yourself Off

Apparently in England we have the most timorous and conservative right-to-die lobby in the world. The kindly Dignity in Dying outfit, which used to be called the Voluntary Euthanasia Society before it was called Exit, a far bolder name, is actually legally unable to give out the telephone number of Dignitas, the agency in Switzerland that helps people bump themselves off when life gets too much.

So what if I just got fed up with living and yet was perfectly okay physically and brainwise? What if I just thought, Hell, you know, actually, I've just had enough. I'm bored with living. I want to try something new? I'd have to do it myself.

I could just take an overdose. At the back of a drawer stuffed with old sweaters and forgotten shirts I have a very, very old bottle of red and green capsules. They must be way past their expiration date, but I hope that by the time I decide to bump myself off they will join the various other over-the-counter drugs that I will dose myself with and add to the lethal cocktail. It's comforting to know they're there, anyway.

Or, if I've lost the pills, which is likely, I could try other methods. Sadly, Dignity in Dying no longer produces a *How to Kill Yourself* booklet —but I was lucky to get their *Guide to Self-Deliverance* (great title!) in 1981. ("You need two plastic bags, approximately three feet in diameter and 18 inches in width. . . . Kitchen bin-liners are an obvious possibility." "For drugs and car exhaust . . . this requires a secure connection between the end of the exhaust pipe and a length of stout flexible hose which should fit over the exhaust pipe—vacuum-cleaner hose appears to be suitable. . . .")

The only problem at the moment is that I've forgotten where I put it.

But I think my loved ones would be very upset and fed up if I went ahead. It's never much fun if someone close to you decides to push off out of choice because it always implies that those left behind weren't loving or amusing enough to make you want to hang around longer. So it would be kinder to one's family for one's own suicide to be arranged to make it look as if it were an accident. I've thought about following fire engines and chasing the firemen (no firefighters in my vocabulary, I'm afraid) into a blazing house, apparently to help rescue the people inside but in fact to incinerate myself along with the residents. Or another way of dying a hero's death would be to adopt an extremely old and disabled dog, with only a couple of weeks to live, throw it into the river, and leap in after it, dying apparently trying to rescue it. It would be perfectly easy to get run over by a police car—I nearly get run over by one accidentally every day—but it wouldn't be kind to the driver. Or of course one could simply take a flight to Zimbabwe and attempt to assassinate President Mugabe. It wouldn't be a bad way to go.

Until Then . . .

Until the time comes for the Grim Reaper to harvest me, there are some amusing things to fritter away the time. I'm quite happy browsing through the obituary columns looking for friends who have dropped off the perch.

Then there's the pleasure of writing one's will. I have rewritten mine several times now, occasionally cutting someone out who has upset

me or putting in someone I briefly love. Sometimes neither, but, rather, leaving the whole lot to saving Romanian orphans. It is a wonderful way of conducting one's emotional life with all the malice and affection released into a harmless document, without ever confronting the beneficiaries (or non-beneficiaries) with one's feelings directly. The fact that usually, after a few months, my will returns to its well-behaved norms doesn't matter. I'll have brief moments of wielding real behind-the-scenes power without anyone ever knowing I've done it—unless, of course, I happen to drop dead in the middle of a family feud or a loopy love affair.

Then you can always organize your funeral in advance. But do it privately. I have often written out the ideal funeral for myself, changing it here and there as a new song becomes my favorite or I swing between fancying a funeral in a church presided over by a vicar with a beard in a dress, and one in a woodland grove presided over by a humanist with a beard in a gray sweater and jeans. But don't dream of giving your notes to the people who will survive you. It will take all the fun out of it for your relatives when it comes to their organizing it themselves (see "Funerals").

And finally—famous last words. Yes, you can start dreaming them up right now. Whenever you wake in the middle of the night, worrying about something, think, instead, of what you'll say on your deathbed. Here are some hints.

Noël Coward said: "Goodnight, my darlings."

John Barrymore: "Die? Certainly not. No Barrymore would allow such a conventional thing to happen to him."

A. E. Housman (to his doctor who'd just told him a good joke): "That is indeed very good. I shall have to repeat that on the Golden Floor!"

Louis IV, to his mourning courtiers: "Why are

you weeping? Did you imagine that I was immortal?"

Karl Marx: "Go on, get out. Last words are for fools who haven't said enough."

Ramón Narvaez, a Spanish general, when asked by a priest to forgive his enemies: "I do not have to forgive my enemies. I have had them all shot."

George Sanders, in a suicide note: "Dear World, I am leaving you because I am bored. I am leaving you with your worries. Good luck."

Logan Pearsall Smith, lexicographer: "Another sunny day! Thank God I don't have to go out and enjoy it!"

And, best of all, Francisco "Pancho" Villa: "Don't let it end like this. Tell them I said something."

6. Sex

As I grow older and older
And totter towards the tomb
I find that I care less and less
Who goes to bed with whom.
        —Dorothy L. Sayers

OH **G**OD! Not sex again! That's how I feel these days when I see that wretched three-letter word looming up at me out of the papers. Honestly, sometimes I think that I've had enough sex to last me a lifetime. Well, I am a bit of an exception, I suppose. As a child of the '60s, hopelessly insecure and depressed, it's not surprising that when I started to add up everyone

I'd slept with the other day and got to—well, I won't tell you how many I got to—I gave rather a shudder and told myself that that was *quite* enough now, thank you, and could we think about something else. Like—er, rhubarb pie. Or how to get grass stains out of aprons.

Anyone who thinks this state of affairs was something to be envied needs reminding that in the '60s no one had heard of the phrase "No means no." We girls got into the most ghastly scrapes. If you weren't raped (and I can think of a couple of times that what happened to me could be so defined), then you were bullied into having sex. I always remember a typical '60s moment when I went out to dinner with a man. He paid. In those days if a man paid for supper, he almost always expected to have sex afterward. It was that simple. He asked me back for coffee and then suggested sex, but when I said I wanted to go home, he looked at me astonished and said, "But why? It'll only take a couple of minutes."

Sex was a kind of substitute for love, and wherever I stand now, or lie (I'm not letting on), I know I'm fed up with sex's lurching longing dominating my life, roaring in my brain when I want to do other things—and I don't mean reading great books or painting great pictures, but just puttering about or mowing the lawn, or finding out the side effects of some new anti-arthritis drug on the Internet. When (rarely now, thank God) I get that clawing feeling below my stomach, aching with want, my eyes don't sparkle at the possibility of another night of leaping about on a mattress. Or, worse, as far as I remember from those heady days, being dragged around on a kitchen table. Frightfully uncomfortable.

No, these days I first of all groan inwardly, and then, when I realize that the feelings aren't so strong that they have to be indulged, breathe a sigh of relief and get on with the ironing. It's wonderful not to have to clamber into bed with some slightly pissed pal or a naïve young pickup, just to satisfy the cravings.

(And I was rather relieved to read that even the great Diana Rigg, at sixty, was recently quoted as saying that although she's quite comfortable with other people of her age having a continued sex life, she herself, although she had a wonderful sex life, is perfectly reconciled and happy "not to go there again.")

Even when I stopped my nocturnal caperings and got back to some kind of sexual normality in the '70s, sex still played a big part in my life as an agony aunt. Until a few years ago, and for the last forty or so years before that, I've been answering readers' problems—and masses of them were about sex. In the '70s we were bludgeoned with advertising about it, told that if you didn't have sex every night of the week you'd become shriveled and repressed, assured at the same time that if you had a great sex life, you didn't need to worry about anything else in your relationship—and there was even a period when simultaneous orgasms, a near impossibility as far as I remember, were touted as the only way of achieving true sexual satisfaction. Men were taught how to have several orgasms a night without ejaculating (that must have required the nerve, mind, and concentration of a sadhu who'd spent years practicing single-handedly at the top of a mountain), and entire books were written about G-spots and H-spots, and how to get rid of spots to attract a man, and whether there was such a thing as female ejaculation, and why anal sex could be a boost for a marriage, and never to rule out fantasies, mirrors, videos, and threesomes. Or foursomes. Or moresomes.

In my time I've written, believe it or not, no fewer than three A–Zs of sex for a variety of publications (*A* is usually for *Arousal,* and we go on through *M* for *Masturbation* and *O* for *Orgasm* until, finally, *Z* for *Zzzzz*—what men do when they turn over after sex). And I can understand the *Z*s. By the time I got to the end of writing each of these supplements, I often felt like having a good old snooze myself.

I tried to calm it all down once, I remember, by answering a letter, in my column, from a woman who said she loved sex but never had an orgasm. What was wrong with her? I replied that she was fine. If she had feelings of closeness, relaxation, sensuality, satisfaction, and fulfillment, then it didn't really matter whether she had an orgasm or not. After the magazine was published, however, I got a letter from another worried reader. "Dear Virginia," she wrote, "I have three orgasms every night. But I never have those lovely feelings you talk about. What is wrong with me?"

It's small wonder that these days, older, wiser, and luxuriating in my single bed, I sometimes thank God that I've been there, done that, got the sexy T-shirt, worn it far too often, and have now given it to the Salvation Army.

I'm with Kingsley Amis who, on being asked at seventy whether he had sex, replied that he was delighted when his libido vanished because he suddenly realized that for sixty years he'd been "chained to an idiot."

Anyway, Who Is There to Go to Bed With?

While I can cope with looking at myself in the mirror with my clothes on, it's not such fun when one's stripped down to one's birthday suit. (Isn't that a sweet old-fashioned expression, by the way? They used to say that in the '50s when the words *nude* or *naked* were considered vulgar.) After all, no one looks absolutely amazing naked after sixty, do they? I don't want to go to bed with a man whose tummy rolls about like another being on the bed. Nor do I want to go to bed with a man whose chest looks like a rolled-down Austrian blind. When I was young, an old friend of mine said, when she got to sixty, "I do think fucking at my age is a bit undignified, my dear." I thought she was crazy at the time, but now I rather agree with her.

When Sex Is Physically Impossible

It's not uncommon for men to find their libidos reduce with age; many become increasingly impotent with weaker erections, and sometimes take longer to ejaculate; some women find sex just too painful to carry on with, however much hormone cream they slather on or however much HRT they cram themselves with. Having sex can sometimes feel as if someone is rubbing you down inside with sandpaper.

At ninety-one, the author Diana Athill said, "One reads from time to time absolutely obscene articles about senile sex—about how if you really go on trying hard enough, using all kinds of ointments, it can work, but for God's sake! It's supposed to be fun! If you need to use a cupboard full of Vaseline, you might as well stop."

We women are always told to "Listen to our bodies. . . ." Well, then: listen. When many older women have sex, their bodies sometimes scream, "Ouch! Ouch! Ouch!"

The Freedom of No Sex

One of the really positive effects of being less interested in sex, is that one can have so much better relationships with men than when one was young. It's wonderful finding that a man isn't scared to be alone with me in case I leap upon him with a predatory roar. Or that I'm not scared to be alone with him in case he does the same to me. It's great that my women friends don't worry, if I go out with their partners when they're away, that I'm on the prowl. Or, worse, planning to steal their partners away. And I've heard that some men actually find women a lot more interesting too, now they bother to listen to them without distraction. Remember the joke about the frog who says to an old man, "If you kiss me, I'll turn into a beautiful princess," and the old man replies, "At my age, I'd prefer a talking frog."

No Sex Doesn't Mean Not Being Sexy

But just because I may be bored with sex it doesn't mean I've turned into some trouser-wearing old bag with cropped hair and not a speck of makeup. I adore looking as glam as possible, love to be told I look young and sexy; I adore flirting, which is all the more fun when you know that it's going to lead precisely nowhere. It's great when you meet a man not thinking, Oh, will he ask me out, will I go to bed with him, could I be married to him? Will I have his children? almost before you've shaken hands. I just love it when "getting lucky" doesn't mean you've scored with a guy but, rather, finding a space in the supermarket parking lot.

Research

Although I'd always like to make the case for ironing as preferable to sex, I can't deny that it's reported that some older people are still at it like rabbits. Even though some of my contemporaries agree with me that the idea of going to bed with anyone even remotely near our own age gives us the creeps—"I suppose I could bear to go to bed with someone of fifty, just, but the catch is that he'd have to be very nearsighted to want to go to bed with me," said a girlfriend—I gather that in Sweden, 98 percent of married men claim still to be having sex *over seventy*. The only way I can understand that is by thinking, Well, that's Sweden for you. Land of pornography, blondes, booze, compulsory sex education in elementary schools—what can you expect? They may have a hundred words for snow in Inuit, but I bet they don't have one phrase equivalent to "Not tonight, darling" in Swedish.

Anyway, when it comes to surveys doesn't *everyone,* old guys in particular, lie about the number of times they have sex?

121

Indeed, many ancients sound rather smug about it all. I feel they're saying, "*That* bit of information will stop them throwing us on the scrap pile! We're just as randy as everyone else!" But I myself don't believe a word of it. True, I don't talk a lot about sex with my peers—people of over sixty like myself—but I strongly suspect it's because sex just isn't remotely as important to them as it used to be when they were younger. I've also noticed that an increasing number of couples not only sleep in separate beds, but in separate rooms. Most, having got divorced ages ago, actually sleep in separate houses.

And I'm sure those who do sleep together certainly agree with the actress Mrs. Patrick Campbell, who said that "Marriage is the result of the longing for the deep, deep peace of the double bed after the hurly-burly of the chaise longue."

Perhaps this is all just my stereotypical English reaction. Perhaps I'm wrong. Perhaps British oldies, too, rather than curling up in their nighties and pajamas after a soothing cup of malted milk, or a stiff double whiskey, are bonking the nights away behind closed doors.

In Praise of Older Sex
If you are one of the people who still enjoy sex despite the fact that these days you sometimes feel you'd like a ladder to help you get up into

bed, there's quite a lot to be said for older sex, which is entirely unlike younger sex.

Your sex drive changes as you get older and can be a lot more unhurried, more relaxed, and less frantic. Indeed, many people say that, being less frequent and more leisurely, sex when you're older can actually be more enjoyable. And because, presumably, couples by this stage know how to please each other, there's less unsatisfying groping and fumbling than there used to be. A sex therapist I know once said that in the case of older sex, "Traveling can often be more pleasurable than arriving." There's also the added relief of knowing that, at last, there is no question of your possibly getting pregnant. It's fantastic not having to take the Pill or, even worse, jamming a rubber cap into yourself every time you have sex. (Remember taking it out? Yikes, as the kids used to say.)

Better Lovers?

Older people can be far more adept at sex. Benjamin Franklin, advising a young man on his choice of mistress, told him, not very flatteringly, about the charms of older women, suggesting that "covering all above with a basket, and regarding only what is below the girdle, it is impossible of two women to know an old from a young one. And as in the dark all cats are gray, the pleasure of corporeal enjoyment with an older woman is at least equal, *and frequently superior,* every knack being by practice capable of improvement" (my italics).

Older people have been around more. Whether older men can or can't last longer, they're certainly far less selfish lovers than younger men. They're more experienced sexually, so there's less fumbling, less blushing, and a lot more laughing. And older men don't go into a sulk if you don't feel like sex or want to watch the end of the TV program before getting down to anything. If they're not confident about their sexuality by fifty or sixty, they never will be. The old gentleman in Sandy Wilson's *The Boyfriend* might have been right when he sang, in a song called "It's Never Too Late to Fall in Love," that love is best when it's old—like wine.

And as for women, there's always Howard Jacobson's view in the *Independent,* which is that "Longevity is more beautiful in my eye. No look can rival for sexual excitement that of someone who has seen the world but still sees something she desires in you . . . Eroticism has nothing to do with youth and beauty but everything to do with intelligence and experience, spiced, preferably, with a little disappointment."

Older men are, of course, far more gallant than younger men, having been brought up in a totally non-PC era. An older man will open doors for a woman; an older man will bring flowers; an older man will tell her how beautiful she's looking; an older man will put on a clean shirt before he comes to visit. An older man will be shocked if his companion hurls her credit card on to the table, insisting on splitting the bill. And finally, an older man always has a place of his own so there's no risk that he might become dependent—always a fear with a gorgeously feckless young man. ("What do you call a musician without a girlfriend? Homeless.")

One friend of mine, after a fling with a dishy twenty-two-year-old, ended up marrying a man old enough to be her father. She said, when I asked what on earth she saw in the bald old geezer, "Not only does he make me feel young, but he's also incredibly grateful that I should deign to go out with him. So I feel not only incredibly attractive, but like a kind and generous person as well. What more could I ask?"

Oh, Yes—Love

Thank God, sex isn't love. I once watched a television program that advised couples on how to rekindle the sparks in their relationship, and I thought, What an utterly crass thing to do. Sparks were then, not now. We've had sparks, done with them. What about the joy of glowing embers instead?

In a wonderful poem, "Kindliness," Rupert Brooke (amazing how he knew this; he was only twenty-seven years old when he died!) wrote of love in old age, when sexual desire has died down.

> And blood lies quiet, for all you're near;
> And it's but spoken words we hear,
> When trumpets sang; when the mere skies
> Are stranger and nobler than your eyes
> And flesh is flesh, was flame before;
> And infinite hungers leap no more
> In the chance swaying of your dress;
> And love has changed to kindliness.

Quite right, too.

7. Recession

One virtue he had in perfection, which was prudence, too often the only which is left us, at seventy-two.

—Oliver Goldsmith,
The Vicar of Wakefield

LIKE EVERYONE ELSE, I've been worrying myself sick about the recession, wondering what's going to become of me and the rest of the world. I thought that in a pinch I might sell the house, get a job stacking shelves at the supermarket. I'd sleep on rich friends' floors, and, finally, jobless, home- less, and pensionless, I'd steal crusts of bread from the mouths of babes to conceal about my person until the moment I could consume them underneath a Thames bridge, in the comfort of my own card- board box.

But one day I woke at about 9:00 a.m.—that's what happens when you take a quarter of a Temazepam (Free! All free!) and a mug of malted milk at 4:30 a.m. because you're so anxious—

and my mind had cleared. I realized that I really didn't need to worry. I was in a very strong position. I had been born, like most of Britain's oldies, in what Cyril Connolly called the Drab Decade. And I knew about recessions like the back of my increasingly liver-spotted hand.

In other words, another great thing about being old is Knowing How to Do Without.

We oldies do actually have a teensy inkling of what hardship means. Well, hardshipish. We know how to eat baked beans out of a can with a comb. Having been born in 1944, I remember ration books. I remember my first banana. And my first avocado pear. (On arriving at *Woman* in the 1970s, when I first became an agony aunt, I found, stuffed at the back of an old filing cabinet, a leaflet to be sent out to readers inquiring what they should do with this mysterious fruit when it first appeared on our shores. It was entitled *How to Eat an Avocado Pear* and started, "Do not eat an avocado like an ordinary pear. . . .")

I remember the streets lined with pen hospitals and doll hospitals, and I remember making do and mending, and sides-to-middling, sheets . . . and it was rather comforting. We used to keep the Christmas paper every year and my mother would iron it to use again the following year. And we had something called a "string drawer" in which bits of ribbon and string, retrieved from the presents, would be carefully coiled and stored.

What We Know That Young People Don't Know

We wait for things to come down in price. We know about supermarket Wednesdays, when all groceries are repriced around five o'clock. We don't understand new gadgets so we don't buy them. Some authors I know still write with a pencil on the back of envelopes. We know about the discount supermarket chain Lidl, and we're not ashamed to shop there.

We know how to make stock out of chicken bones. Indeed, we actually know how to cook! Which is more than a lot of young people know. We know what "leftovers" are, and how to make a meal from the leftovers of yesterday's leftovers. I know that it's best to go to the market on a Saturday evening to get cut-rate vegetables, and I seem to remember once eking out a big chicken for nearly a week . . . first roasted, then cold with salad, followed, the next day, by the rest of the bits all deviled . . . and finally made into the most delicious stock that provided the base for a hearty soup that lasted for two days.

We know that if the cheese grows a strange green bit on the side, we just slice it off. We understand what is meant by the term *fly-walk*. We know not to worry our heads about use-by dates, best-before dates, and sell-by dates. Smell-by dates, that's more like it. Younger people who look in my cupboard are always shocked to find yogurts or packs of lentils way past their sell-by date—and look very wary when I tell them that this is exactly what they're going to have for their supper.

I had a bit of pork the other day that was looking a little green about the gills, gave it a good scrub under the tap, cooked it for hours, and it was absolutely delicious. I know you may now be thinking, "We won't be going to supper at her place," but when bread costs $10,000 a loaf, you'll be glad of a bit of green pork at my house.

It is second nature for me to turn out the light and close the door every time I leave a room to keep the heat in, and I know not to fill a kettle too full if all I need is a cup of tea.

As for heat, when it comes to getting dressed I understand the principle of layers and, indeed, if I scrabble about far enough in my chest of drawers, I could actually come up with an undershirt and a pair of very warm long johns. I do *not* find it odd or humiliating to be caught cooking in a pom-pom hat, a pair of mittens, a woolly vest, and a pair of warm boots.

I can darn socks. I know what a darning mushroom looks like. I know not to eat it like an ordinary mushroom. I cut off old buttons from unwanted clothes and keep them in a button box. I can turn cuffs, *and* I can then boil the buttons up to make soup. You get the idea.

Dressmaking

My mother cut costs in her day by making pencil skirts when new material was thin on the ground—and then, when the New Look came in, she made glorious little black Dior dresses with huge full skirts out of cheap blackout material. In the '60s I used to make very fashionable minidresses by buying old gentlemen's undershirts and dying them purple. I still have the urge sometimes to go out dressed only in an old Turkish carpet. With the right accessories I feel pretty sure I could get away with it.

Weird Tips

During the recession of the '70s, I asked readers of a column I was writing to give me some examples of money-saving tips. I knew of course about storing old bits of soap, boiling them up, putting them in a tube to set, and making new soap out of the result—though I found it rather revolting. I myself invented an infallible way to make my tights last twice as long: cutting off the leg with the run and wearing the good one with another single to make two.

But I wasn't prepared for the bizarre. One reader told me that rather than throw an old sweater away, I should sew up the neck, cut off the sleeves, thread elastic through the bottom, and bingo! Warm woolly underpants for winter! Another told me of a cunning way to fold paper to avoid the need for an envelope; another advised me to chop up old rubber gloves from the fingers up in thin strips and "Presto! A year's supply of rubber bands!"

As for the problems of next Christmas, I have already kept, in my "present drawer," unwanted presents given to me from Christmases past ready for recycling next year.

In my part of London, Shepherd's Bush, where a lot of Polish refugees live, I am used to seeing old people collecting bits of wood from construction sites to take back to hoard in their gardens. It is the habit of a lifetime and I am considering not only joining them but elbowing them away when I see a good bit of timber going to waste.

New Things

We oldies don't need new things, do we? I remember when I got a new stove the other day and a friend said to me, "Well, *that*'ll see you out!" And it's true. I've got enough stuff to *well* see me out. I doubt if I'll ever need a new ironing board. Or a new stepladder. Or a new electric drill. And there will no doubt come a time when a new toothbrush will see me out, too. I've got a lot of what is currently known as "stuff."

Free Things

We get so much for free now that we're old. Reduced entrance to museums and galleries and cinemas. A pension! Then they put £200 a year into my bank account for heating without even so much as a by-your-leave.

Not to mention free eye tests—I'm always at the optician's asking for another one—*and* free prescriptions. And then, if you live in London, you get a free travel pass. The day I got mine I was like a child. I hopped on a bus and went one stop—flipping a mental finger to everyone else on it—and then I took the bus back home and did the same again, back and forth all afternoon. It didn't cost me a penny.

We've Scrimped and Saved

Now, I know that many of us find that we're not as well-off as we thought we would be. But most of us oldies have *something* stashed away if we're sensible. We possess the "silver pound" (I don't like calling it the "gray pound"—sounds so depressing). In fact some of us have quite a few silver pounds. The over-sixties actually own four-fifths of the nation's wealth. And the great thing is that since we're not going to live much past eighty-five (please, God, in my case), we've only got a limited number of years in which to spend our cash. Many of us find we are actually miles richer than we ever were before in our lives.

One reason we're lucky is that we've never been of the borrowing generation. We disapproved of the first credit cards, particularly the one that claimed to "take the waiting out of wanting." We're used to waiting. And waiting. And waiting. And often if we wait long enough, eventually we discover that we don't want what we thought we wanted after all. Or, at least, by the time we start thinking of purchasing it, it has hurtled down in price. Or become obsolete.

And even if we're not rich, all of us know how to make something out of whatever we've got left.

Lodgers

Many young people wouldn't dream of taking in lodgers. I wonder if they're even called "lodgers" anymore, actually—the word is reminiscent of dusty bank clerks, wending their way up stairs covered with threadbare carpets, guttering candles in hand. But the moment I've had a room free in my house (and a house is something you often find you have, when you're old, which is a bit of a treat), I've always stuffed a lodger into it and, in times of recession, I'm sure I could accommodate a couple of families in the cupboard under the stairs.

Eeyore Mentality

We are hardened to hard times. We don't expect a lot. We were children during the cold war, and to some extent most of us have adopted some kind of deep-grained nihilism; that is to say, what's the point if we're always four minutes from a nuclear holocaust? At the same time cynicism and skepticism inform our psyches, too. It's not because we're selfish that so many of us can't be bothered to recycle, and hoard our incandescent lightbulbs despite the threat of global warming. It's because we've lived with changing threats all our lives—from the idea of hell, foisted on us at Sunday school; to the Bay of Pigs and nuclear war; to the world being wiped out by AIDS, then bird flu—and we've heard the cry of "Wolf!" too often to believe it.

Growing Our Own

Some of us have bits of land on which to grow vegetables. And having been laughed out of court as we used to stagger home with our baskets of tomatoes, reduced to making tons of green tomato chutney in old Nescafé jars, we now have so much produce the laugh's on us. Soon we'll be able, perhaps, even to barter our beans and peas for services, or sell them on the black market. And once the house is packed to the rafters with lodgers, we can always retreat to live in our shed on the allotment, just returning home occasionally to have a bath and collect the rent.

They do say that the only people who survived the Irish potato famine were those with turnips and shotguns, so once I've got my hands on a shooter, I'll turn my garden over to vegetable production, put a barbed-wire fence around the edge, and retreat to the shed, making only occasional forays out to spend all the cash I've amassed under the fold-up bed.

Back to Childhood

Isn't there, for those who remember penny-pinching times in the '50s, something rather comforting about a return to frugality? I'm not talking about it being comforting for anyone on the breadline or who's at risk of losing their home, but for the reasonably well-off middle class, the sort who might buy this book, there is something rather cozy and reassuring about the idea of toasting crumpets in front of a blazing (as opposed to electric) fire (which, of course, we know how to make) and following it up—because we Know How to Make Our Own Entertainment—with a game of charades, or a round of cards.

And because in Britain we're not a generation that has realized itself only through shopping or, like the young, has no reference to our existence except what we saw the previous night, we have many more resources than they do to keep us going. It is possible to spend a very pleasant evening simply reading a good book.

I've often felt like an alien in a world of bling

and choice; I'm baffled by women who possess five hundred pairs of shoes, or even more than about six (and that would include slippers), come to think of it. I've shopped in my time, but I've never shopped till I've dropped. Old people, on the whole, just don't. Lucky us.

They say that "by the time people have money to burn, the fire has gone out," but that's fine. Let's just put on another shirt. Or sweater.

Or, even better, some weird nightcaps we've knitted with the wool unpicked from a couple of old tea cozies.

8. Work

At sixty-three years of age, less a quarter,
one still has plans.

—Colette

IF, ALL YOUR LIFE, you have felt utterly humiliated by having to reply, when asked what you do, with the words, "Shelf stacking at a supermarket," you are now in the wonderful position of being able to answer instead, "Well, actually, I'm retired." It's a very crass person who will then ask what you are retired *from*. And if they do, you can just airily brush them aside with a groan and a "Don't ask . . . the traveling . . . the meetings . . . thank God it's all behind me." They are not to know that the traveling involved taking the train from Greenford to Wood Green and then a bus, every day. And the meetings? Nothing more than directing people to the butter.

It can be pretty much of a shock when you stop working. What are you going to do with all that time?

Generally, however, after the initial shock, we usually find we're busy with things that we actually want to be doing, rather than with a job that, while fulfilling in some ways, may well have involved hours of pointlessness and boredom. One of the great things about being old is that you're your own boss and you'll never have to go on one of those frightful bonding team-building weekends ever again. Okay, you miss the camaraderie and the gossip around the water-cooler, but isn't it a pleasure not to be play-ing Secret Santa ever again? Isn't it a treat never having to open a present of a willie-warmer and pretend to find it incredibly amusing? Isn't it great never having to look again at a flowchart or welcome focus groups from other countries or attend all those grisly going-away parties that take place before your own? Isn't it fantastic *not* to feel part of a team made up of members only half of whom you have any time for?

But if, as Noël Coward said, you find that "work is more fun than fun," dealing with retire-ment may be a matter of trying to pretend that what you're doing in your leisure time is actually work. (And let no one pretend it isn't. Anyone who has tried to organize a village fete will sometimes long for the unchanging, straight-forward hours of the office.)

You could, of course, pretend to continue working. No, I don't mean like that Sherlock Holmes story where a man used to leave his home every morning dressed for work and then, a few streets away, change into ragged clothes, smear his face with coal, and spend the day begging in the Strand. No, I mean you can take on unpaid work and treat it in exactly the same way as you used to do your job. If you have special skills, there are charities desperate for free advice, apparently. Or, I suppose, if you were desperate, you could actually work for money, by stacking shelves for one of the few firms that actually create special job opportunities for oldies. Don't forget: Winston Churchill was sixty-five when he first became prime minister and started his epic struggle against Hitler (who was in his forties).

Or you could do volunteer work. The problem with volunteer work is that it is, these days, no longer a matter of sauntering into a place and lending a helping hand. You nearly always have to have some kind of training for voluntary work, and commit yourself to various days or evenings. If you're working with people, you're usually checked to see if you have a criminal record and frankly, it's often too much of a hassle, since you can feel hampered at every stage of the way by people who resent unpaid amateurs coming in and doing their jobs—often better than they do.

However, you might get lucky. But when I offered to mentor young people in my area—a job at which I knew I would excel—and they heard my fluting, upper class South Kensington tones, I was told sharply that there was nothing available.

I would recommend if you're good at work and want to use your own skills, be admired, interact with other people, but never feel under too much pressure, that you become a local do-gooding busybody. If there isn't a Residents' Association on your street, set one up. If there is one, join it and push your way up to becoming the chairperson. Sit on the local police committee. Involve yourself in Neighborhood Watch. Keep your eyes peeled for unsuitable planning applications and, if everyone agrees, object to them, and set up petitions, marches, meetings, and demonstrations. Be a pain.

Write to the papers. Challenge parking tickets. Buy a litter stick and go down the street every Sunday, picking up trash and ostentatiously putting it into the garbage cans. Watch from behind your curtain to take down the van numbers of builders who come and dump trash on your street. Pressure the city for a recycling bin. Pressure the city to remove a useless recycling bin.

By setting up our own antitram group in Shepherd's Bush and combining with other groups along its proposed route, our residents' association managed to help stop a plan for a tram to run down our main thoroughfare, a plan devised by our then mayor, Ken Livingstone, not a man who was usually thwarted in his ambitions.

You may become something of an irritation, even become known as a meddlesome old fart, but you will find that it's a great way to get to know everyone on your street, to wield some influence, and, however much people resent you in some ways, your role can only be a force for good in that you will encourage everyone to get to know one another and feel "part of a community," as they say.

It's not work as you knew it—but it's work.

9. Downsizing

Eighty years old! No eyes left, no ears, no teeth, no wind! And when all is said and done, how astonishingly well one does without them!

—Paul Claudel, *Journal*

WHEN YOU GET OLDER everything diminishes. Or should diminish. And it's rather a nice feeling. Instead of having a desire to conquer empires, you long to reduce yourself and your surroundings. You don't want to expand, you want to contract. I don't see it as something depressing. I see reducing as being like something you do to a wine sauce. From being all sloppy and tasteless to start with, after you've simmered it for ages, it eventually turns into a delicious, pungent concentrate.

Not for us oldies the idea of shopping till we're dropping. Not only are we, if we're lucky, reasonably replete both materially and emotionally, but we also know from long experience that buying more stuff won't make us any happier. It will just mean we will have less room to move and more things to dust.

I couldn't help but note, when I recently went on a cruise (see "Travel") that when all the oldies poured off at the ports, they avoided the souvenir shops and sellers of trinkets around the harbor. "I have," said one of them to me, sighing, "enough Russian Matryoshka dolls. I have enough castanets. I have enough pottery peasants with pottery straw hats sitting on pottery donkeys. My aim is to bring absolutely nothing home with me at all except the clothes I brought with me."

Ask any oldie what they'd like as a present, and nearly always their answer is either a consumable or something with a short life span. Flowers. Bath oil. Tickets to the theater. Marrons glacés. Plants. Room spray. Candles. A useful can of moth repellent. What you just *don't* want is something to keep. Because this is an age when, curiously, you realize that it's true that you "can't take it with you." As a result you have far less attachment to things. And having spent most of your life acquiring things, it's tremendously exhilarating, now you're old, to get rid of things. Quite honestly, when one of my grandsons breaks some precious ornament, I'm secretly rather relieved. It means that another bit of baggage (as one's past is now known) has been thrown into the garbage can. And, as a result, some of the burden of owning possessions has been taken from one's shoulders.

I have an idea that Buddhists eventually want nothing but their prayer mats, and I find discarding things rather a freeing exercise, myself.

I used to take photographs of everything. I have two whole drawers bursting with albums all marked with dates and years. These days I can hardly be bothered even to pack my camera, far less actually get it out to take a picture. I honestly can't see the point.

Now, this is the moment when you may think of moving. Of course you may *have* to downsize because you're releasing capital by moving into a smaller, more manageable, place. (But for pity's sake, beware of moving to a bungalow. A bungalow can knock years off your life. Doctors say that the best place for a retired person to live is in a very thin eighteenth-century house positioned at the top of a steep hill—walking up and down keeps them fit.)

But where to move? When they were younger, lots of my friends imagined that when they became older, they'd retire to the country. A few of them have indeed done just that, but not as many as those who've lived in the country all their lives and who decide to spend the last years of their lives in cities or large towns. In urban areas there's more efficient transport, more friends who live nearby, and the medical services are usually much better and closer.

Once you've found your smaller house or apartment, you can start to get rid of things in a big way. Perhaps it is now time to throw out that funny old massage machine you bought at a "Mind and Body Show" twenty years ago. To get rid of the rusting extra bike you have in the shed that you're keeping for a guest to ride. To realize, now that your fingers are starting to seize up, there's really no reason to keep that ancient Spanish guitar you bought in the '60s hoping to impress your friends with flamenco songs. And now's the time to start transferring, if you have the expertise, all your old singles, EPs, and LPs onto CDs at last.

And while you're at it, now's the time to spend a bit of money on getting an appraiser to come to your house and find out what everything really is worth—sparing your offspring the ghastly task of doing the same when you die. You can give your children things in advance, too, things that might prove a bit of a liability when the probate comes. And you make sure that you've destroyed all those embarrassing letters and disks that have evidence of a life you might not wish them to come across when you're dead.

Do they really want to know quite how much you missed them when they left home? Or how painful you found it when they forgot your birthday? Would they appreciate finding love letters from a woman who wrote to their father *after* he was married rather than before? Would it be useful or kind to allow them to find the birth certificate of a baby you had given up for adoption when you were young and foolish? Or the fact that you had once had cancer, got over it, and had never told them a thing about it? Now you can rake over the old traces and leave the past a pristine area, devoid of skeletons in cupboards.

And isn't it just *wonderful* not to have that awful possessive anxiety that you used to have about objects? The very phrase *"Mine!* It's *mine"*—a phrase that, I'm ashamed to say, has been constantly on my lips from the age I first could speak—is one that I hear myself saying far less frequently, and certainly less stridently. "It's mine . . . well, sort of mine . . . well really, it's ours . . . what the hell, why don't you have it? Who cares?" I find myself saying more and more often to my younger relations.

I never thought that to give more often than to receive would ever bring me such unconditional and easily achieved pleasure.

10. Looks

Then, seated on a three-legg'd Chair,
Takes off her artificial Hair:
Now, picking out a Crystal Eye,
She wipes it clean, and lays it by.
Her Eye-Brows from a Mouse's Hyde,
Stuck on with Art on either Side,
Pulls off with Care, and first displays 'em,
Then in a Play-Book smoothly lays 'em.
Now dextrously her Plumpers draws,
That serve to fill her hollow Jaws.
Untwists a Wire; and from her Gums
A Set of Teeth completely comes.
Pulls out the Rags contriv'd to prop
Her flabby Dugs—and down they drop.
Proceeding on, the lovely Goddess
Unlaces next her Steel-Rib'd Bodice;
Which by the Operator's Skill,
Press down the Lumps, the Hollows fill,
Up goes her Hand, and off she slips
The Bolsters that supply her Hips.
With gentlest Touch, she next explores
Her Shankers, Issues, running Sores,
Effects of many a sad Disaster;
And then to each applies a Plaister.
But must, before she goes to Bed,

Rub off the Dawbs of White and Red;
And smooth the Furrows in her Front,
With greasy Paper stuck upon't.
She takes a *Bolus* e'er she sleeps;
And then between two Blankets creeps.
—Swift, "A Beautiful Nymph Going to Bed"

I'M A REAL LOOKIST. I'm not saying I look great all the time, but I do think it is one's moral duty not to look too ghastly. Looking good lifts not only your own spirits, but also other people's as they see you walking down the street. So, in my book, looking one's best is actually good manners.

There's no excuse, when you're old, to "let yourself go." And yet so many people do.

Visit any service station along the highway and what do you see? Hordes of old people who've simply not bothered to do anything about their appearance when they got up that morning. The women have opted for a frightful kind of cropped haircut, which needs no more maintenance than the odd clip, like a hedge, possibly by the local council; they haven't bothered to put on any makeup and, often, they're wearing the asexual uniform involving some kind of amorphous "top," a Windbreaker, and underneath a pair of tracksuit bottoms, socks, and the ubiquitous sneakers. Some women just seem to have given up being women completely—they look just like lumps on legs.

I know what they'd say if I criticized them for looking so utterly dreary. They'd say, "But I just want to be comfortable." But it's perfectly easy to be comfortable in a much more attractive getup.

And anyway, however comfortable you want your clothes to be, you don't want to *look* as if your clothes are comfortable. I remember a member of the audience, a friend of an actress appearing on stage in a play, who had to visit her in her dressing room after what was an excruciating performance. After wondering whether to lie through his teeth or tell her the truth, he settled on a line that got him off the hook. "Darling!" he said, kissing her on both cheeks. "You looked as if you were having a *marvelous* time!" In other words, "You were thoroughly enjoying yourself! But everyone else in the audience was bored stiff." So whenever anyone says of your shoes or your clothes, "They look as if they're really comfortable," it's time to rush back home and change into something that looks as if you've taken a little bit of time and trouble.

And the men—what's happened to them? Presumably when they were young they took some kind of pride in their appearance. But now nearly all of them have tummies the size of space hoppers, some of them haven't even bothered to shave, and it's not because they want to achieve some kind of fashionable look. Go to France and you'll find a completely different picture. Whatever age anyone is, the vast majority take care with their appearance. And it shows.

Friends of mine have asked me, "What's the point? I'm completely *invisible* now that I'm older. I'm all wrinkles. I've lost my looks." But I say that a good-looking oldie can have the time of his or her life, particularly in England. The standard of looks in England is, like the standard of food except in the cities, so low that with only the minimum of effort you can stand out as some kind of ancient Marlene Dietrich figure. Or Tina Turner. It just takes a bit of flair and courage.

You don't want to aim for the BUPA look, of course. That's the one cultivated by the couples who model for brochures for private patients' plans. They usually look eerily young, and yet they both have full heads of slightly tousled graying hair, they often wear his 'n' hers Wind-breakers, and he always has his arm around her shoulders as they gaze unflinchingly into the hazy middle distance, as if on a mildly breezy head-land. These pictures always give a sense of coast-lines and imminence and a vague idea of Cape Cod and clapboard. He may have a windlass, suggesting access to yachts (and therefore to funds), while she may be gray-haired but wears just enough lipstick to suggest she still kicks up her heels when the urge takes her. Sometimes they are pictured on a golf course, or wandering through an autumnal wood (get the point?), eyes sparkling, their faces full of fresh hope and with rather stupid grins because, presumably, they know that when the need comes to have their hips done, BUPA will pay.

Then there's that picture of that immaculately permed lady on her stairlift. And that rather elderly model with the snow-white perm in the small ads at the back of the *Telegraph* magazine, who is always lying at the bottom of her stair-case pretending she's "had a fall," clutching the emergency call button around her neck and hoping desperately that someone will come soon.

I have never seen people like these "old" models in real life, and I certainly wouldn't want to look like them.

To a degree, of course, there's not a lot you can

do (apart from having major construction work on your face) about your basic look. For instance, like many people, I realize that the older I get the more I look like my mother. Oscar Wilde once wrote that it was every girl's great tragedy to "become like her mother." But my own mother looked pretty good. Even when I was a child, people used to say, "You can tell you're mother and daughter! You're as alike as two peas in a pod!"

When I was older, taxi drivers used to take us for sisters. My mother would simper and fumble in her bag for an extra-large tip.

We each fiddled with our hair; we have such similar voices that when I hear old tape recordings of the odd radio interview she gave, I could swear it was me speaking. We both have large breasts and a right-footed bunion. And we both have dark hair and drooping eyelids that give us a slightly Asian look; the same retroussé nose, the same big mouth. When my mother was fifty-four she had cosmetic surgery on her eyes—she was starting to look rather *too* Asian—and when I was fifty-four, after a friend at a party said that I looked like a Burmese princess, I had an eye-job as well. When my mother was fifty-six she had a proper face-lift, and got the incipient wattle ("the lizard look," as she called it) removed from her neck. When I was fifty-six I had exactly the same operation.

And now, after trying to get away from the boyish haircut that my mother insisted I wore when I was young—"It looks so French, darling," "But I don't want to look French! I want to look English!"—I have finally given up growing my hair, putting it up, curling it, wearing it in a bob; realizing she was right after all, I have resorted to the short gamine style that she knew suited me best all along. A cut just like hers.

How can you improve your looks so that you can look even better in old age than you did when you were young? Some of my friends, it's true, have certainly been dealt what in France is called a *coup de vieux*. One day you see them and they look halfway reasonable, the next you can barely recognize them. It's as if builders had come in the night and suddenly removed an I-beam in their face. Everything turned to a pile of rubble. Total collapse.

But their collapse is everyone else's gain, because it means that those of us (yes, I'm that vain I include myself) who bolted themselves against the wreckers stand out even more. And, to be honest, even those with wobbly window frames and in need of a bit of repointing do look more "themselves" than they ever did. Their crow's-feet and laughter lines and wobbling necks can conspire to make a face that looks a great deal more individual and original and approachable than it ever did in the days of peachlike skin and silk-spun hair. It's all a matter of how you deal with the situation.

Now, there is a line between looking an utter wreck that's completely gone to seed and looking like a latter-day Joan Rivers, hair so well done and makeup so perfect that you suspect it's been imposed by a fairy godmother and come midnight, the whole edifice collapses. Yet if you try, you can become as striking, outrageous, or subtly elegant as you like without too much cheating. As Eleanor Roosevelt said, "Beautiful young people are accidents of nature but beautiful old people are works of art."

And you can, really, look much better when you're old than when you were young. Many's the old person whose striking looks have prompted me to think, Gosh, they must have looked wonderful when they were young, only to discover, when I see the photographs, that they were then just boring blobs, indistinguishable from other young people of the same period.

None of us wants to look old in a horrible way, but we can look old in a good way. No one wants to look like a vandalized 1950s community hall in Hull, but I wouldn't mind looking like Tintern Abbey. Or the Temple of Karnak, come to that. Indeed, a very fashion-conscious friend of mine even looks in shop windows for clothes that she might buy in advance of the moment when the going gets tough. She has a couple of what she calls "cancer hats" that she thinks she'll look good in if she is ever forced to have chemotherapy. And the other day she came around in a newly bought coat that she wasn't sure whether she liked enough to keep; as she twirled in front of me, she said, "But maybe I will keep it after all. It would be a very good funeral coat."

In order to look good when you're old you must, however, obey some basic rules. I'm passing on the following tips, given to me by my mother, who knew what she was talking about because she was professor of fashion at the Royal College of Art in the '60s and helped put people like Ossie Clark on the map.

1. Never wear white, particularly near the face. It makes yellow teeth look yellower and the whites of your eyes will show up as slimy gray with streaks of red.

2. Always keep your upper arms well covered. Those bits of flesh that hang down at the sides (known, apparently, as "bat wings") are hideous—and so are those strange rolls of flesh that appear between your underarms and your body.

3. To be honest, I'm not really too keen on glasses with strings. I know everyone has them, but they do look . . . well, a friend said they make people look deaf (see Hearing in

"Ailments"). They always remind me of those little kids you used to see with string threaded through their coats to keep their gloves on.

4. Get a new bra every six months at least and keep it well hitched up. You don't want to be one of those people whose boobs touch their tummies when they sit down. Or, worse, when they stand up.

5. Don't disguise a lizardy neck with a scarf or polo neck. They look as if you have something to hide—and the imagination always conjures up something worse than the reality. I'm always reminded of neckerchiefs whenever I'm driving past a line of Leylandii trees. Rather than thinking, What a nice bit of greenery! I think, What monstrous building are they trying to hide behind that wall of pine? A nuclear power plant? A prison? The British branch of Guantánamo Bay?

6. Always be *spotless*. It's funny: young people can wear filthy old garbage bags and shoes with holes in them and still look great, yet an old man wearing an immaculately cut Savile Row suit, shoes sparklingly polished, a crisp white, starched shirt, but with a tiny speck of egg on his tie looks utterly repulsive. And if you have to wear pants, always check the bottoms of them. It's amazing

how the bottoms of trousers can catch a puddle when out in the rain, and by the gravity-defying power of photosynthesis (I think) the stain then creeps *up* the trouser till it's nearly at the knee. (To be sure, I'm always droning on with my "spotless" line to people and then find later I've got some ghastly butter stain on my skirt.)

7. Unless you really are superfit or some ancient athlete, don't wear sports clothes. They just draw attention to your lack of muscle tone.

8. If you feel you have to wear a copper bracelet to ward off rheumatism, keep it well hidden under long sleeves. Old crock you may be, but there is no need to advertise it.

9. Wear comfortable shoes by all means but don't wear shoes that *look* comfortable (see above), particularly anything that involves Velcro fastenings.

10. If you've got any old Ossie Clark dresses hanging in your wardrobe or now-fashionable vintage bell-bottoms from the '70s, why not try them on? If they're too small, either lose weight or get them altered so they fit. You'll look utterly gorgeous.

11. Make sure you possess and wear the most glamorous dressing gown in the world. Because in the future, when you're lounging around in an old people's home staring into

space, you're going to be spending a lot of time in it.

12. Have a face-lift. When talking about the joys of looking good when you're old, I'm often accused of hypocrisy because I've had one. But I didn't have it to make me look younger—honestly! I had it done because, after years of depression, I just looked so incredibly miserable. When I got up in the morning and looked at myself in the mirror, even I was brought down by what I saw staring back. It didn't reflect the more optimistic person I now felt inside. Even when I smiled I looked miserable. I'd kind of cried my face into shapes of gloom that depressed myself and other people. And when I'd had the operation, no one told me how young I looked. They all said simply how *well* I looked. Much nicer.

13. Try not, unless you have a figure like a sylph, to wear pants. As they age men tend to appear more feminine, while women, with deepening voices and hairs sprouting out of their chin, tend to appear more masculine. Don't encourage the slide by dressing to look like a guy. If you're a woman, I mean. The older you get, the more feminine you must try to look.

14. If you're a woman, don't skimp on the makeup. Not only does your face look better

with it, but it declares to the world that you've made an effort. And that is flattering to everyone who spots you, even total strangers in the supermarket or those odd people with whom you connect briefly when you spot them at the wheel of the car next to yours. (Speaking of makeup, have you noticed that even though it makes no difference at all now, because your skin is so nonelastic, you still make that funny pulling face when you put on your eye makeup?)

15. If you are a man, please, I beg you, *do not grow a beard*. They look like small sheepdogs hanging on to your chin. They also announce a) that you have a problem with your masculinity and b) that you have no interest in giving oral sex. Also, I do find that every gray-haired man with a beard does, these days, bear a remarkable resemblance to the notorious serial killer Dr. Harold Shipman.

16. If you're a man and your hair is thinning, *emphasize* it. Either shave your head completely, or just get a normal haircut. (Do not ever, ever be tempted to drag a piece of hair over your head from one ear to the other, with a parting just over the tip. It may look reasonable to you in the mirror but, I can assure you, from the back it looks repulsive.) Also, never grow your hair long when you're

old. There is something immensely depressing about the sight of long, straggly gray hair on a man, especially when dragged back into a sad old ponytail. Far from looking like a cool old groover, you look like something from the '60s washed up on the beach, something that's hung around in a rock pool for a very long time.

17. Never wear anything that looks as if you are going on safari.

18. If you're a woman and your head looks like one of those old scrubbing brushes with only a few bristles left that you occasionally find down the back of the fridge, for God's sake swallow your pride and get a wig. After a long course of steroids, my hair was thin and peculiarly curly, so, sweating with embarrassment, I visited a wig shop and took the plunge. I even wore it a few times. They're not vastly expensive—you don't need real hair—and, although they are excruciatingly hot and uncomfortable, and feel rather as if you are wearing a bathing cap (an odd experience as you sit in a nightclub at two in the morning), after a while you do get used to them. Joan Crawford wore them. And if she can, you can.

19. Mouths are particularly important to address when you are older. As far as teeth go, I wouldn't encourage you having them

whitened (see rule 1). But watch out for crowns. Sometimes your teeth gradually get yellower and yellower, leaving a few gleaming crowns, which only make the other teeth look worse. At least ensure your teeth are all the same color. Floss often. This is particularly important since, as our gums recede (hence the phrase "long in the tooth"), there are tiny gaps at the tops of our teeth just made for catching spinach, raspberry seeds, and bits of toast. Make sure, too, that your tongue is clean. Some old people have tongues covered with a kind of whitish gunge, which, while not noticeable to them when they admire themselves in the mirror with their mouths closed, is repulsive for other people to spot when they're talking to them. Tongues can be cleaned by covering them with bicarbonate of soda and then giving them a good scrub with a toothbrush. And, finally, don't forget to check the sides of your mouth. Some old people have little bits of dried spittle at the corners of their mouths. This is totally disgusting. If you have this problem, keep a hankie in your hand and wipe your mouth constantly.

20. If you have a paunch, don't worry too much. Everyone has a slight paunch after sixty. And no amount of sit-ups or exercises will make any difference. I once went to an

exhibition called Age in London, knee-deep in Arrange Your Own Funeral Parlors, Time-Shares in Spain, splendid chairs that rose up and down and flung out footrests at the flick of a switch, forms for writing your own will, stands advertising private health plans, and men in suits eager to flog insurance of every kind. A saucy sideline was an exhibition of the oldest muscleman they could find. He was eighty years old, quite wrinkly, covered with fake tan, and with admirable biceps and pecs, but I was reassured to see that even he, who no doubt worked out every day of his life, had more than a slight paunch. However, even though paunches can't be helped, it's a good idea to conceal them as far as you can, even if you have to pour yourself into slimming panties when you go out.

If you still think it's impossible to look good when you're old, listen to what Howard Jacobson wrote in the *Independent* about Leonard Cohen:

a devilishly attractive man in his middle seventies. Some men do old age better than they do youth. Especially melancholy sensual men who can't decide whether they're happy or not. The not knowing, like the not eating, keeps them lean. He is fascinatingly attenuated, as laconic as a snake on grass, with a face lined and amused by a desperate indulgence of the appetites, by which I don't mean wine, women, infidelity and betrayal, but also with rhapsodic spirituality alternating with ecstatic doubt.

If you're a woman and can't face the huge effort required to look good in old age, you can, of course, simply give up and look totally bonkers —much better than being invisible. You can cultivate the Batty Look. Now you're old, you can get away with preposterously wild colors, layers of silk and gold, flying scarves (as long as they're clean), and enormous straw hats covered with a pyramid of flowers, apples, and pears. Don't worry about being extreme. You're confident enough, now, aren't you?

You may look crazy, of course, but you can also look incredibly pretty at the same time.

11. Young People

When I was young my teachers were the old,
I gave up fire for form till I was cold
I suffered like a metal being cast.
I went to school to age to learn the past.

Now I am old my teachers are the young.
What can't be molded must be cracked
 and sprung.
I strain at lessons fit to start a suture.
I go to school to youth to learn the future.
     —Robert Frost, "What Fifty Said"

WHEN I WAS YOUNG I hated old people. I hated their wobbly old lips, their leaking

eyes; I hated their smell and I hated their wrinkly old hands with all those rivers of veins. I also hated the way they dressed and the fact that they had nothing in common with me whatsoever. Not only that, but they were utterly baffled by me and my generation. Like all young people in the '60s, I was a complete mystery to older people. We were, after all, a generation that had been pretty much invented by the '60s. Okay, there were the bright young things in the '20s, but they belonged, as far as I can gather, exclusively to a certain class. The new generation of "swinging" young people in the '60s could come from any class at all, and preferably not that of the oldies of my acquaintance.

There was a social revolution going on and the old were utterly mystified as to why I, a middle-class girl, was hobnobbing with criminals and sleeping with East End boys, who turned into designers, photographers, entrepreneurs. The media were also rather irritatingly fascinated. As a pop columnist for the *Daily Mail* in the '60s I was constantly on hand to explain the workings of the Young Person's Mind to anyone older than me. I remember having to do a Young Person's Dictionary for the old geezers who read the paper, which gave explanations for words like *square, cool, fab, trendy,* and so on.

I remember I'd be sitting at a party and some ancient old crock would come staggering up and sit down next to me and say, "Oh, *hello!* I so wanted to meet you because I do so *love* young people. Tell me—why do you wear your skirts so short and why do the Beatles wear their hair so long? Shouldn't it be the other way around? Ha ha ha!" and I could feel her secretly plugging an invisible socket into my side and sucking all my youth out.

The first thing to be said about growing old is that nobody does it deliberately in order to annoy the young. I only understand that because now I am myself old. These days no one calls me to ask about why young people like to take drugs. They call me to ask what my views are on Alzheimer's research, or whether sex is better when you're ancient, or whether, as an old person presumably on the point of death, I approve of euthanasia.

I'm in an odd position. Because on the one hand, the old really *are* different now. There may be an element of self-deception going on here, but I know that the cultural gap between me and a young person of thirty is far smaller today than it would have been between myself as a thirty-year-old and someone of sixty-five when I was young. In fact, I have probably done more drugs, slept with more men, and, crucially, experienced far more change in my lifetime than any young person born in the '80s or '90s. At the same time I remember the days of trams and when businessmen wore bowler hats and carried rolled-up umbrellas. My generation has witnessed a huge cultural shift, which means that we are in a special position of being able to understand the very old—those of ninety or so—as well as understanding the young.

I can't deny that I am, at the same time, an old geezer; there are things about the young that I just haven't got a clue about. Nowadays when I hear the word *hip,* I don't think of some cool groover in tight jeans, but more of the possibility of a fascinating operation that I can learn something from. (Though I was rather amused in a shop when a very young person, to whom I gave the right change, replied "Fab." I stared at her, wondering if she wasn't actually someone of my age who'd had several face-lifts, but no. She was twenty. Apparently *fab* is coming back. Cool. But you have to be very careful of what old slang you revive. If you describe yourself as *square* and the young person you're with as *swinging,* I think you'd soon find they were looking at their watches. Or whatever they use for watches these days. Cell phones. Chips in their wrists.)

The fact that this distance between young and old, while it still exists, has narrowed since I was young, makes relationships with young people far easier than they used to be. And the presence of young people in our lives means that the horizons of our friendships are immediately widened. When we were young we couldn't have relationships with younger people because we were all young. But now I love having a semimaternal role with anyone young. Even when I was fifty, young people could be seen as a slight threat, but now that I'm sixty-five not only are they no threat to me, I'm no threat to them. I'm not going to steal their boyfriends or their friends or betray them by repeating gossip. I'm safe. And, embarrassing to admit, I just love them.

Now, some old people can't stand the young. When comedian Frank Carson, who is now eighty-three, was asked what he thought of today's comedians, he replied, "I hate them all —particularly Jack Dee and Jimmy Carr. Because they're funny, much funnier than me, and so *young*." And the actor Richard Griffiths said he thought everyone over fifty should be issued by the post office every week a plastic bag with a wet fish in it so that "whenever you see someone young and happy you can hit them as hard as you can across the face. When they say 'What was that for?' you'll say 'For being young, handsome, and successful.' "

But I just *love* young people. And it's so incredibly flattering, too, to be liked back by a young person—any young person. While I used to boast that Mick Jagger had once kissed me (on the cheek, admittedly, but a kiss all the same) I now boast about the ages of some of my fiends. I was asked to go to Italy last year and when people inquired about it I said, "Sicily . . .

but you know the person who's invited me is very young. She's thirty-four. She's a friend of mine, you know. . . . Yes, and *she asked me to stay*. She *likes* me. She's very *young*—younger than my own son, and she's this thirty-four-year-old, did I mention her age?—and she's asked me, so much older, to Italy to *stay with her*. . . ." I behaved like someone who'd been invited to dinner with some rock star. I felt flattered and flirty and lucky.

The young are like a drug to the old. And it doesn't matter how young, either. When I was young I'd be wheeling a carriage down the road with a baby inside it minding my own business and out from behind a bush this frightful old bat would leap. "Oh, coochie-coo! What a lovely baby! Isn't he bonny! Or is it a she?"

These days, I find myself behind a bush, minding my own business, when down the road comes a young mother with a baby in a carriage and I'm the one who leaps out crooning, "Oh, coochie-coo, girl or boy? What a bonny little person!"

The great thing about being old is not just that I can have young friends, but that I still have friends who are older than me. And when I'm with them, I feel like a little girl. I sit at their knee and ask them about their youth, and I'm genuinely fascinated by their stories.

Howard Jacobson, himself no spring chicken, wrote in the *Independent*:

Myself, I love the company of people who are 'past it.' Doesn't matter what the 'it' is, particularly. Being past anything is enough. The commonality of self-irony is what I like. The absence of any of that competitiveness that mars the lives of the active . . . I like being with people who weren't born yesterday . . . The acceptance that we are among the ruins . . .

Then there's also the fact that we can *hear* the most interesting young, those who spend their lives in noisy clubs; they tend to shout quite naturally because their ears are already damaged with exposure to overly loud sound. And those less interesting, of course, are still delightful. As someone said, "What music is more enchanting than the voices of young people, when you can't hear what they say?"

I have friends of my own age, my peers, whom I can talk to as contemporaries, but now there's this new type of semiparental relationship I have with young people. I don't think any young man knows how deeply flattering it is for an old person to be deemed worth spending more than half an hour with. When she was old, my mother used to come to life whenever a young man crossed her path. She turned embarrassingly girlish and flirtatious, completely energized by the presence not just of a young person but a young fellow. Humiliatingly, I find it hard not to act the same. I only have to catch the eye of a young man in the car next to me, and if he gives me a smile, I find that when I finally reach my destination I am dancing on air.

It's not just that young people are nice to have around. As our old friends drop off their perches, we *need* young people, just to replenish the supply of friends who seem to diminish daily. Every day, new names are crossed out from our address books.

In Holland, the Dutch are apparently building an entire town for the over-fifties. Senior City in Zeeland will have no schools, dance clubs, or tattoo parlors, and motorbikes will be banned.

I have to say that it sounds like my idea of utter hell.

12. Travel

When I was very young and the urge to be someplace else was on me, I was assured by mature people that maturity would cure this itch. When years described me as mature, the remedy prescribed was middle age. In middle age I was assured that greater age would calm my fever and now that I am fifty-eight perhaps senility will do the job.

Nothing has worked. Four hoarse blasts of a ship's whistle still raise the hair on my neck and set my feet to tapping. The sound of a jet, an engine warming up, even the clopping of shod hooves on pavement brings on the ancient shudder, the dry mouth and vacant eye, the hot palms and the churn of stomach high up under the rib cage.

In other words, I don't improve; in further words, once a bum always a bum. I fear the disease is incurable.

—John Steinbeck,
Travels with Charley

LOTS OF US have lists of "things we want to do before we die." The late Miles Kington wanted to learn how to yodel, whistle with two fingers, and how to pronounce both the words *macho* and *chorizo*. Others want to see the world and check out all those places they've always meant to visit but haven't had time for. So, at the top of the list of things to do for most oldies, if they've got enough money and have retired, is to travel.

It strikes me as an odd thing to do. Traveling is what we do best when we're young—it's natural for youth to look outward—and surely, like a dying leaf curling inward, it would seem to me to be more nat-ural to travel *less* or at least *nearer* when you're old rather than more and farther. But again, it seems there's this desperate trend for oldies of my generation to refuse to acknowledge that they're getting on. Far from relaxing into themselves and enjoying the fruits of their labors, they long to have a final fling, as it were, and fly till they die.

However, oldies aren't dumb. You don't find many of them hitching around Europe or taking jobs as washer-uppers in Paris bistros and cattle-ranchers in Australia, as many young people do in their gap years. No, oldies like to travel in comfort.

Cruises

Cruises are just bursting with ancient people, all eager to squeeze through the Corinth Canal, float through the straits of the Bosphorus, nip around the Mediterranean cities, marvel at the fjords of Norway, or sail around Cape Horn *before they die*. Cruising also suits old couples. If he's too old to master a boat trip of his very own, there's nothing an old fellow likes to do more in the morning than stand on the poop deck, stuffed to the gills with a three-course breakfast, and watch other guys weighing anchor and splicing the mainbrace or whatever they do. And their wives, of course, can sit in the "well-stocked library" researching whatever pile of historic rubble is on the list to see that day.

Anyway, the rub about cruises and old people is that so many other oldies have the same idea. And I don't know about you, but I don't want to be trapped on a floating prison with dozens of people with crutches all over the place. People of *my own age*. On one cruise I went on—I was giving a talk—they actually had a mortuary on board, which, when we finally disembarked two weeks later, was packed to the portholes with fellow cruisers who couldn't make the distance.

(I also don't want, incidentally, to sleep in a room the size of a small coffin in a bed the size of a schoolgirl's pencil case, nor do I especially want to learn Flower Arranging on the lower deck portside on Friday afternoon, nor indulge in Scarf-Tying Class on Monday morning in the Royal Tea Lounge on the Promenade Deck— "Discover how to wear scarves effectively to suit your own style and enjoy the hands-on experience as you learn lots of chic knots and tying tricks." Don't get me started. . . .)

Some cruise lines are so anxious not to become floating nursing homes that they oblige passengers to sign a piece of paper in advance saying that they are fully mobile and able to take part in the visits and won't hold anyone else up. But you can hear the grinding of the cruise line people's teeth as they witness the crippled masses who lurch aboard waving their passes, all claiming that they had to have a hip operation, or slipped on a banana peel, *after* signing the contract. Life on a cruise hardly helps general mobility either, because you get so little exercise. And you do nothing but eat on a cruise, four meals a day. They say travel broadens the mind. But it also broadens the behind.

I was told of one old lady whose feet, during the last years of her life, barely touched dry land. Between cruises she'd put up at a hotel in Portsmouth so she had time to cash in her vast collection of prescriptions, before sailing off to her next destination. ("Another truss, Lady Bonkers?" I can imagine the pharmacist saying.

"And your usual bunion splint? That'll be free for you, since you are over sixty. And by the way, I do like your new Chinese hat. Suits you very well.") I think the cruise people were trying to get her banned, because you don't want someone wandering off unable to remember her name when you're trying to keep everyone together on a crowded visit, say, to the Taj Mahal. If she got lost, you would simply never find her again.

Trekking

When I heard about oldies going on trekking holidays abroad, I wondered if they weren't the type of a slightly more adventurous nature. Apparently Dame Freya Stark was eighty-eight when she set off pony trekking in the Himalayas. But it's not for me, for many reasons. First, I don't really like walking (see below) and also, if I were to fall off the trail and break a hip (see Balance in "Ailments"), I wouldn't really like my skeleton to be discovered years later beside some Yeti bones. But finally, when I investigated further, it turned out that my old friends didn't *really* go trekking at all. Well, they did, I suppose, but they might just as well have been walking up and down their own living rooms for all the effort it cost them. Apparently, they had teams of slaves crashing on ahead to build little tents and make steaming suppers for when they arrived, and dozens of donkeys carrying their bags—not what I call trekking in the Himalayas; it's what I call a Big Cheat, frankly. Next thing they'll be telling me all about the perils and excitement of deep-sea diving and it'll turn out that they haven't been doing anything much more adventurous than going upstairs and having a bath.

Walking

Proper walking is frightfully popular with oldies in England. Appropriately enough, it's called "rambling." Loaded up with special sticks, stout shoes, and clipboards and compasses hung around their necks, their backpacks stashed with provisions and water bottles, they stomp around in the Lake District wearing out the land with their hobnailed boots. Of course, I have to bow to their crazy doggedness, their delightful Englishness, their utter devotion to total pointlessness, but I myself have never really understood walking as an occupation in itself. It's rather as if someone told me that they went "breathing" for a fortnight.

Gap Years

I have heard of a Web site for *real* oldie adventurers, called Gaps for Grumpies; the idea there is that fit old people take gap years (gap between what, I wonder—retirement and death?) and buzz off to African villages or Peruvian farmlands, and help with such things as painting schools, building wells, and teaching people to read. Now, this appeals. Because it's not just a way you can travel if you want to, but also a way you can actually use your age and your wisdom to do something useful. I haven't tried this, but when I am less busy I plan to give it a go. No, really.

The Panic of Flying

Of course, there might be a slight problem for me. How do you get there? That seems to me another disadvantage to foreign travel when you're older. Forget the ethical problem—I'm a nonbeliever when it comes to greenhouse gases, carbon footprints, and global warming—I don't want to fly simply because these days I get too flustered. Being flustered and being old seem to be synonymous. It's a funny thing, but alongside the huge and increasing confidence in many areas that comes with age, in other areas lots of oldies, I in particular, can become gibbering wrecks.

The last time I drove to Stansted to catch a plane, I missed the highway exit and had to carry on to Cambridge and back before I could find it again, adding thirty miles to my journey and, worse, a panic-stricken hour eating into the check-in time.

More recently, having arrived at Terminal 5

(which had hidden itself in ill-signed networks of roundabouts and slip roads), when the woman at the check-in desk said, "And how are you today?" I simply burst into tears. And I mean *tears*. I couldn't speak and had to sit on a bench gasping and choking with misery, holding my head in my hands. And when, on another occasion, at Gatwick, I was told to "check yourself in," I simply had a nervous breakdown.

"I can't!" I said. "I'm too old and I *don't understand!*"

Luckily a kindly man in a uniform did it for me, but he admonished me, as I thanked him. "You'll have to get used to it," he said, severely. "This is the future."

Well, if this is the future, that's the last time I go abroad, I thought.

Like all old people I get muddled at security, often putting my water, nail scissors, and little pocketknives into a plastic bag in full view of the guards who always confiscate it, and taking off my skirt instead of my boots at the X-ray machine . . . and the last time I went through I actually tried to put on someone else's belt and shoes after they'd come off the rollers.

Hotels

We oldies need to be in charge. Which of course makes staying in hotels so problematic. Whereas when I was young I could check into a hotel, throw my suitcase into my room, and then hurtle down to the beach, now every time I stay in a hotel, I have to spend about an hour tidying my room after breakfast and doing a bit of light housekeeping. The day I check in, I put all the hotel gunk—plastic folders, little cards saying "No Smoking," and unwanted electric clocks—into a drawer, rearrange the chairs, unpack (but don't put anything in drawers in case I forget it when I repack), make sure the towels are arranged in the way I like them, check the heating system and the phones—and usually tear all the bedclothes off the other single bed, if there is one, and pile it onto mine so that I'll be warmer at night. Each evening I do my washing and hang it to dry on the shower curtain. The last time a friend of mine visited me in my hotel room she said it was like entering a Turkish bazaar, everywhere draped with tights, swimming costumes, slips, sarongs, and underwear.

Trains

Of course I could travel the smart way: by train. And a year or so ago I did manage to go from London to Moscow entirely by train (never again). Sadly, trains are a grisly form of transport these days; the last one I went on had a guard speaking sententiously on the intercom before we left. "I would like to point out that this train has special facilities for your feet," he said. "It is called the floor." While I'm normally tolerant about other people's behavior I find that just being in a train car turns me instantly into an old grump. Why is he speaking on his cell phone in a Quiet Carriage? Is the seat beside him really taken, as he claims, or has he just put his baggage there to give himself more room? Train cars induce a kind of incandescent fury.

Biking

I would go on a biking holiday, but since I was told by a cycling instructor that now I was so old I couldn't turn my neck as far as I used to be able to and therefore biking was, for me, rather dangerous, I've put my helmet and yellow jacket away. Though I suppose if I were brave enough I could buy a trike. I see fearless oldies triking away—although now their form of travel is more likely to be those reckless little buggies used only, it seems to me, not by the disabled but by the hugely *fat*. (Can anyone tell us, what is the law on those things? Are they really allowed to travel both on the sidewalk *and* the roads?)

Driving

So it's the car for me. I don't actually own, as my great-aunt did, an old Ford, with little yellow indicators that flicked out on either side when you were turning left or right, and a cranking handle to wind up the engine; hers was so old that she actually had to reverse it to go up steep hills. Nor do I possess such a thing as a driving hat, and there isn't a driving blanket in the back. But I don't yet have central locking and my windows are wound up and down by hand.

My only indulgence is a brilliant gizmo, installed following the frightful disaster driving to Stansted and Terminal 5: GPS. Not only can I now get from place to place without risking a heart attack (see "Ailments") but also, if by any chance I am driving with a loved one—and I do *have* loved ones, despite my insistence on spending most of my time alone—there is no risk of incurring the most almighty row that usually, as far as I remember, resulted in night after night of the silent treatment when we actually arrived at our vacation destination. Women have always wondered why men don't ask for directions when they lose their way. Now neither of them has any need to. They are told where to go as they go along by a disembodied voice sitting on their dashboard.

England

I've made an extraordinary discovery since I've gotten older: there are dozens and dozens of absolutely sensational places in England that I haven't been to before. Someone said that "at sixty, a man learns how to value home," and I'm starting to realize exactly what he meant. Why go to Italy when you can go to the Lake District? Why trek in the Himalayas when you can walk in the most beautiful scenery in the world, in Inverness-shire? Is there really anywhere more staggering than the Cornish coast? Anywhere with more amazing birds than Norfolk?

Travel of Another Kind

Finally, for us of a certain age, there is a kind of existential Proustian travel that appeals to me most of all. You do this from the comfort of your own bed. You wake up, having endured the long journey of sleep the night before, and then, hour after hour, you trace, with your index finger, a slow and meditative path along your sheets and quilt, acutely aware, wherever you are, of the changing colors, whether you're going up or down the folds in the coverlet, occasionally glancing up at the ceiling to check out the cracks, and sometimes, on a hill of pillow feathers, glancing around to take in the view of a glass of water, false teeth, unreadable book that you couldn't get beyond two pages of (leave that Book Club!), stack of pills, dressing table, hairbrush, mirror, wallpaper, and so on. Some people have managed to travel like this for weeks on end.

Try it.

13. Funerals

Lately there's nothing but trouble, grief, and strife
There's not much attraction about this
      bloomin' life
Last night I dreamt I was bloomin' well dead
As I went to the funeral, I bloomin' well said,
"Look at the flowers, bloomin' great orchids
Ain't it grand, to be bloomin' well dead!
And look at the corfin, bloomin' great 'andles
Ain't it grand, to be bloomin' well dead!"

Some people there were praying for me soul
I said, "It's the first time I've been off the dole"
Look at the mourners, bloomin' well sozzled
Ain't it grand, to be bloomin' well dead!
Look at the children, bloomin' excited
Ain't it grand, to be bloomin' well dead!
Look at the neighbours, bloomin' delighted
Ain't it grand, to be bloomin' well dead!

"Spend the insurance," I murmured, "For alack,
You know I shan't be with you going back"
Look at the Missus, bloomin' well laughing
Ain't it grand, to be bloomin' well dead!
Look at me Sister, bloomin new 'at on
Ain't it grand, to be bloomin' well dead!

And look at me Brother, bloomin' cigar on
Ain't it grand, to be bloomin' well dead!

We come from clay and we all go back they say
Don't 'eave a brick it may be your Aunty May
Look at me Grandma, bloomin' great haybag
Ain't it grand, to be bloomin' well dead!
"Ain't It Grand to Be Bloomin' Well Dead!"—
written and sung by Leslie Sarony in 1933

AREN'T FUNERALS *FUN?* Apparently there are many people who enjoy funerals and memorial services so much that they pretend to have known the late lamented just in order to go along to the bash afterward. Victoria Coren wrote about this gang who tried—and succeeded —to gate-crash the memorial service of her father, Alan Coren. I'm tempted to hire this lot in advance for when I die, plus, perhaps, a few actors who will be paid to droop around the place, sniffing their misery into hankies and occasionally emitting the odd wolflike howl.

It's interesting that I haven't noticed anyone clamoring to get into anyone's wedding.

And I know why. I've worked out scientifically —yes, scientifically—why funerals are so much more fun than weddings. If you take a handful of marbles and lay them out on a table, and then add another handful, which is what happens at a wedding when two families meet at the reception, all the original marbles are spread farther apart. But take the same group of marbles and remove one from the middle—as happens at funerals—and everyone gets closer together. Funerals are warm, affectionate affairs with everyone thinking good things about the person who's gone, feeling closer to those who are left behind and, often, quite smug that, for the moment at least, it's not them in that box over there.

It's also a time to count who is left, who is still there on your side of the river Styx. Dreary old relatives, whom you might have taken somewhat for granted in the past, suddenly look warm and sparkling. They may not be soul mates, but at least they are still here. They are alive, they're not dead, and they probably love you, as you love them, in that peculiarly loyal and dog-like way that relations love one another.

I like the music, the hymns (except for when the organist strikes up some tune other than "Crimond" for "The Lord is my Shepherd"), I like the speed—cremation services, particularly, usually last no longer than half an hour—and I love the cadences. Funerals usually start off sadly, and then build up to a rousing finale, when we all look around at one another congratulating ourselves on having survived and secretly wondering at whose funeral we will all be meeting again in the near future.

And we all leave saying effusively to one another, because we wonder if we'll ever see them again, "I *love* you."

The Downside

Let's put aside the grief, which is not the correct subject for a book that's supposed to be celebrating the great things about being old. Apart, then, from the non-Crimond music there are only two things I dislike about modern funerals. One is the habit of organizing one's funeral in advance, thus taking all the fun out of it for your bereaved relatives. I got a letter the other day from an insurance company.

"Dear Ms. Tronsde," it began.

It's never easy to imagine the time when you'll no longer be here to help and support your loved ones through life's ups and downs. But the simple truth is that one day, there's one challenge they're going to have to face without you. Arranging the

funeral of someone you love can be difficult and distressing. As you try to come to
terms with your loss there are suddenly
endless practical arrangements to make,
such as finding a funeral home and arranging the wake. And the cost of it all can be
unexpected. It's the last thing your family
will want to deal with, yet it has to be done.

I screwed up the letter and threw it into the
waste basket. Total trash. Arranging a funeral
isn't difficult or distressing. On the contrary, it's
a real pleasure to organize things when someone dies. It gives you a sense of control, a feeling
of *doing* something for the person who's gone,
and it also gives you something to take your
mind temporarily off the disaster that has just
befallen you, so that you're not completely over-
whelmed.

Poring over previously unread Bibles, searching for suitable quotes, telephoning vicars to ask
about hymns, discussing tunes with organists,
making out the guest list and wondering whether
to ask an aunt loathed by the deceased but who
would be mortally hurt not to be invited, discussing with undertakers which size of coffin to buy
—all these may be interesting, therapeutic, and
even amusing. (I won't forget the undertaker
who came to visit us before my father's funeral
and who, on being told my father had done

some designs for glass engraving in his time, nodded his head; so used was he to the jargon of his trade that he commented, "Grave englassing? That sounds interesting.")

Bickering—or agreeing—about the music and the readings and the venue is a great way for families to get back to normal life. Uniting in hatred of some harmless figure in the whole scenario—often the poor old vicar or fatuous organist—helps make everyone feel a weird kind of togetherness when a family structure is damaged.

The second thing that ticks me off about modern funerals is when there's a funeral dictate that says: "No flowers." Or, worse, "No flowers, but contributions to Charity X."

The one thing I am going to say in advance of my funeral is that there are to be no "No" anythings. If people want to dance on my grave, fine. If they want to sacrifice young goats on my funeral pyre, that's up to them. If they want to say the Lord's Prayer backward as they throw earth into the hole, let them. And if they cover my coffin with masses and masses of cut flowers, well, that would be best of all. How people pay their respects to the dead person is up to them, not up to the puritanical wishes of those arranging the event.

Aren't flowers at funerals lovely? To ban them makes it seem as if flowers were an unseemly display of fun or attention seeking. The grim old coffin can be covered with them and, at its best, you'll find every variety there, from grand florist's bouquets to the wild roses plucked from the dead person's favorite bush, to the touching bunches of weeds contributed by grandchildren. And surely, aren't cut flowers to do with sacrifice, part of a pagan urge that we all have to give something to the dead person purely as a gift, something that is no use to anyone else? Flowers are like that mindless spraying of a champagne bottle after a Grand Prix victory—an offering up, a giving with no receiving. A check to the Red Cross, decent as it may be, just gets in the way of what should be a private, loving gesture from you to the one you loved.

I like what my grandmother used to call a "good" funeral—big, dark affairs, with glossy black horses hired to parade from the dead person's home to the cemetery—preferably with the words *The Champion* spelled out in flowers along the side of the coffin carried in a huge glass hearse. Splendid.

Undertakers

The last undertaker I had dealings with was dressed in a vest, tie, and black suit, and found it hard even to smile. I imagined undertaker-training classes in which they are tickled and barraged with jokes, and the first one to crack his poker face and smile is kicked out of the course. The moment we were in his parlor it was like being transported into another age, apart from a bizarre bright metal coffin in the window. ("There's a sprung mattress inside," he assured us.) No computers here. Everything was written down laboriously in longhand. Words like *catafalque* and *committal* were used, and I remembered a time when I'd been asked to write a client brochure for a large American funeral company entitled *How to Arrange a Funeral*. There were only two problems. They didn't want the word *body* to be used. They preferred *the deceased*. And they recoiled at the mention of *ashes*. "What word should I use instead?" I asked, baffled. "Cremains," was the memorable reply.

At that point I put my foot down.

Leafing through a brochure in the funeral parlor, I saw that we could order a coffin with a photograph printed on the side—a country scene, golfing paraphernalia, a rocket, you name it, there was one. There was a rock 'n' roll one, a jazz one or even—really creepy—a coffin that was painted entirely with the Union Jack. Apart from a vaguely heathery one with a picture of the Highlands, there didn't seem to be one appropriate for the middle class. The problem is that it's only after you've signed and sealed the whole ludicrously expensive package—around $6,000 inclusive of limousine and hearse—that you remember the Natural Death Centre, who'll organize a woodland funeral in a biodegradable coffin. Next time, I always say to myself, rather ghoulishly.

Memorial Services

If you really want to gild the lily, you can, a month or so after the funeral, organize a memorial service. This can be worked on for much longer by the family, who may have been too dazed to choose much more than a kind of Chinese set meal of a funeral from the church's menu. "Crimond"? Yup. "Love Divine"? You bet. John 2:23-6? Sure, whatever you say. And some prawn crackers and a pot of jasmine tea while you're at it.

A memorial service is usually a celebration of a life rather than a mourning for someone who's gone. After it you all come out thinking what an enormously good fellow he was, the one who's died—and aren't we incredibly lucky and, of course, clever, to have managed to have been his friends? As we leave we can, as we do so often when we're old, congratulate ourselves.

My Fantasy Funeral

I'm torn between wanting a ceremony in Westminster Abbey featuring a choir of white-robed eunuchs who, after the service, release flocks of doves from cages and announce a public holiday, followed by burial in a vast mausoleum topped by a giant marble obelisk; or the Alison Uttley (the British author) version, in which my body is laid in a mossy woodland grove in a hand-painted cardboard box under a weeping willow, where rabbits and squirrels and birds, peeping out between the daffodils and tulips, will weep at my passing.

Oh, Gawd. Sobbing at the idea of my own funeral. How delightfully self-indulgent can you get? Pass the Kleenex.

14. Boring for Britain

When I am an old man I shall bore people.

When I am an old man I shall bore people—
Strangers on trains, in pubs, on street corners
In all weathers, with rambling accounts of
     how life used to be.

I shall rehearse to all in earshot my hard-won
     prejudices,
Or boomingly declaim odd scraps of half-
     remembered verse
By Kipling, Housman, Tennyson, and Larkin.

Clearing crowded carriages with rant,
Banging on about the young and the dead and
The gilded dullards who populate the present.

In ratty egg-stained tie, half-mast trousers,
     undone fly,
Unkempt, unshaven, eloquent and *right*—
About whatever subject takes my fancy.

I'll blather on contentedly about
The weather, noisy music, gormless telly,
The price of fish, the lack of common courtesy.

Slurping discount gin and gobbling pills
And telling all and sundry of my ailments
In graphic, unscientific detail.

Buttonholing the unwary passerby
With unverifiable monologues
Of how things were in my day.

I'll garrulously repeat off-color jokes,
Blasting my interlocutor with rancid breath
The spittled punch lines wheezily forgotten.

Then droning on about myself, myself, myself,
Knowing what licence folk will grant old age
When howling rage seems sour grapes merely.

I really ought to get in training now,
So friends who know me won't flinch in dismay
When suddenly I am old, and start to bore people.
                    (With apologies to Jenny Joseph,
                    author of "Warning")

WHEN YOU'RE OLD you reach, at last, your anecdotage. This gives you permission, as far as I can see, to bore anyone within hearing distance completely rigid for the rest of your (or possibly their) life. A curse for them but, no question, a great pleasure for you.

   I used to be rather wary about boring people. Too much rested on my being entertaining and listening and making the other person not only feel that I was interesting, but also making them, with the aid of a lot of "Ohh!"s, "Aaah"s, "You don't say!"s, "My goodness, that's fascinating"s, and "You certainly have made a really good point there"s, feel interesting. But occasionally now I sense those polite inhibitions breaking down. I get that old Ancient Mariner feeling creeping over me, hold whatever poor sap has come into my range with a glittering eye, and start on a subject—probably something that happened in the old days—and I go on. And on. And on.

The joy is that there's so much that young people don't know these days! They show a distinct lack of curiosity in things that predate themselves. (Just the same as I did when I was young.) Did they know that George Formby was big in the Soviet Union? Did they know that Norman Wisdom was renowned in Albania? Did they know that Jimmy Clitheroe was huge in Africa? "You don't know who Jimmy Clitheroe was. . . . Well, let me tell you . . . he was a little guy who dressed up in shorts, with a cap, and he pretended to be young and he had a voice like this. . . ." The eyes of your listener may glaze over, but there's no stopping you. Imitations of every old comedian you can remember start pouring out of your mouth. I even "did" Max Miller for an unsuspecting young person the other day, even though Max was long before my time. And I have no idea what he sounded like.

Most young people don't know anything about anything, barely know who Anton Chekhov was, and certainly haven't read any Leo Tolstoy. And if you describe a figure as Rubenesque, they look at you goggle-eyed: "Yer what?" And this means you can drone on for ages about topics not only that they don't know about but also, if you're lucky, that you don't know anything about at all either.

You can start quite honestly: "When I was young we didn't have computers, we had things called typewriters—you put the paper in, rolled it up, and at the end of a line—*ting!* And we didn't have photocopiers either, oh no. We got these huge bits of waxed paper and typed on them and if we made a mistake, we had to correct them with little spots of liquid wax . . . and when I was a child I had to go to the fishmonger's and collect huge slabs of ice to break up and put in our icebox, we didn't have fridges then, and when I was a girl, a man would come around every evening on a bicycle holding a stick with a spark on the end of it to light up the gas street-lamps. . . . I remember the day when the only fruit for sale were oranges and apples, and you had to buy your olive oil at the pharmacy. Garlic was unheard of, and there were no microwaves . . . oh, the fog! And of course no single woman was allowed to take out a mortgage in those days. . . .

"You won't believe this, but there were people called bus conductors in those days, and they punched little colored tickets . . . and no cell phones or even answering machines. If we expected a call, we just had to stay in and wait for it. . . . There were no supermarkets, no high-ways, no tea bags, no instant coffee, no sliced bread, no frozen food, no flavored potato chips, no vinyl, no CDs, no Pill, no sneakers, no Starbucks . . . can you imagine it? Of course you can't."

Then you get on to the half-truths. "There were no antibiotics when I was young—you could die if you got an infection" (well, there were a few, when I was a little older than very young). "And of course the sound of bombs was deafening" (well, I don't actually remember the sound, though I was born during an air raid). "And then when we were called up . . . oh yes, it was hard in the trenches in the war. I was in the Women's Corps and the first night I found myself in no-man's-land. . . ." (entirely untrue, but irresistible now the audience is quite spellbound). "And it was there that I had my first roasted rat. . . ."

The young seem to think of the past as a totally other country, and have no concept of the difference between the two world wars. I sometimes feel I could claim to have been at the Battle of Hastings, leading a troop of archers, and the innocent faces of the young would still be gawking up at me, thinking, She must be very old . . . but still, it's amazing. . . .

And of course, those who know perfectly well that you're talking complete nonsense will be far too polite to dream of correcting you, simply putting you down as a loony old fart.

You can indulge your grumpiest and most curmudgeonly of feelings and tastes simply because you're old. You can go on for hours about whether the best way to Basingstoke is on the A40 and then down past Stonehenge—"dreadful what they've done to it—I remember when you could go up to it and wander around touching the stones"—or whether it's quicker via the M4, taking the Salisbury exit. When you stay away, you can insist on having the same breakfast every morning on the grounds that "that's what I always have for breakfast." You can insist on arriving at opening time at the post office and forming an orderly line. You can salute the drivers of AA vans and get irritable when they don't respond as they used to in the old days.

You can say, "I never go to McDonald's," or "I never sing in church," or "I never send Christmas cards," or "I never buy the *Daily Mail*," or "I never watch television," as if these are principles that actually make up an unswervingly upright character that, whatever happens, could never, ever change. (My own feeling is that the rigid views of the old arise simply from fear. If they stick with the views they've always had, they believe, then they won't get carried away by the terrifying eddies and pools of what they see is the chaos of the modern world.)

Even the comparatively young Cosmo Landesman said, in his memoir *Starstruck*, having made some rather grumpy comment:

It's when I write things like that that I start to wonder: Am I being nostalgic for an age that never existed? Am I talking about the state of England or the state I'm in? Maybe it's just me getting old and becoming a grumpy old guy who thinks everything is getting worse. But if this were true you could never make any critical judgements about aspects of contemporary life, because you'd always end up accusing yourself of being a grumpy old guy or woman when, in fact, you could be dead right about what is really going on.

This is precisely why it's such fun being an old bore. Because there's always a chance you might just be right. The world really *might* be coming to an end. If I had a hot dinner for every time I've heard, over the last few months, people declaring that we are behaving like the people in the last days of the Roman Empire, I'd be so fat I'd have to be winched out of my window on a hoist every time I wanted to go out to get my free pills at the pharmacy on a free bus.

As for the perennial topic of young people, possibly top of the list in the Old Bores Subjects charts, you just have to read part of the Reverend Henry Worsley's prize-winning essay, "Juvenile Depravity," written in 1849—though, to be honest, it could still be used perfectly well by an old bore of 2010. Juvenile depravity is, he wrote,

a bane to society, which like an ulcer on the body is continually enlarging, and distrib-uting far and wide its noxious influence—a general and latent depravity, which a large extent of juvenile depravity seems to indicate, is a state under which the manufacture of a nation must eventually decline, agriculture languish and commerce disappear. The number of juvenile offenders, whose precocity in wickedness is subject of grief and alarm to every well-regulated mind . . . the overwhelming mass of vice and crime, now deluging our land . . . the increase in degeneracy of the juvenile population . . . the current of iniquity which at the present sweeps through our streets . . .

Now we could learn from him. When it comes to being an old bore, he really takes the cake.

15. Alone Again

I thrive best on solitude. If I have had a companion only one day in a week, unless it were one or two I could name, I find that the value of the week to me has been seriously affected. It dissipates my days, and often it takes me another week to get over it . . .

I do not know if I am singular when I say that I believe there is no man with whom I can associate who will not, comparatively speaking, spoil my afternoon.

—Henry Thoreau, *Journal*

NOW ONE THING is absolutely certain. Either you're on your own, or you're "in a relationship," as they say. And even then, unless of course you die first or both drive off a cliff in the same car, you'll be alone at some point in your life. Even if you've had a marriage as long as Lord Longford's, there will be a time, after death has come knocking, when one or the other in a partnership has got to live by themselves. It can be a scary thought, particularly if you've been with someone else for years.

And yet being alone, though not easy, is not the end of the world.

I am here not to point out the drawbacks, of which there are myriad—including, of course, tremendous feelings of isolation—but rather to highlight just a few things that are *nice* about being on your own. And a few thoughts on how to stop screaming in agony if loneliness comes up and bites you in the heart.

The Pleasure of Not Having Someone Else Around

I had a small party of about twenty-five people recently and, as she said good-bye, a friend added, "I *so* enjoyed myself. It was such a success. And do you know why? There were no *couples*."

She was right. There were two gay couples, and two people who'd only just started living together, but there were no actual couply couples, people who have grown into each other like ivy into a tree.

I hasten to add that most of my couply friends seem, amazingly, to remain individuals in their own right, even after years of marriage, but I've met some of the ivy/tree variety. Couples who go shopping in the supermarket together every

Saturday. Couples who, when they go out to a dinner party of several people, insist on Sitting Next to Each Other. Worse are those couples who are so intertwined that what started years ago as private bickering has now become public. The ones who call each other "darling" all the time. People who individually are delightful, kind, and funny, and who turn into squalling monsters when they're combined.

"I think you're wrong, darling," says one to the other. "It was Wednesday." "No, love of my life, it's you who've got it wrong. It was Thursday." "I hate to contradict, sweetie," replies the other. "But you're getting a teensy weensy bit muddly-upply in your oldie agie. I know it was Wednesday." "Don't you muddly-upply oldie agie me, light of my life," counters the other, getting really edgy. "I have my diary to prove it." And then, through gritted teeth, "My *angel*."

It's at that point I feel like screaming, "For fuck's sake, who cares if it was Wednesday or Thursday! Just get on with it!"

They're the type who, when one tells a story, make frequent corrections to the flow. Sometimes, before the first person has barely even started the story, the other shouts, "For God's sake, that's the punch line! Don't start with that! You've ruined it already!" Or the other, at the very end of some long saga, when they've been interrupted a dozen times, sighs, "Who's telling this story, you or me?" You thought you'd invited a pair of lovebirds around to your place; instead what you got was a bare-knuckle boxing match.

One of my friends whose husband has retired says that she is infuriated by the sound of his step on the stairs at around noon every day and hearing the words, "What's for lunch, pet?"

"I married him for life, and not for lunch," she says, shuddering as she speaks, moaning about having him around all day. I don't like to tell her that that situation will, one day, change.

It's at times like these I thank God that, despite huge bouts of loneliness lurching into my life over the years, I am, for the moment, single. And I suspect, too, that at moments like these, the individual partners must, for a moment, just a fleeting moment, wish their partners would simply vanish in a puff of smoke.

Then there's also the horror of actually having to sleep beside someone night after night. It's not just because physically sleeping together isn't as enticing as it used to be. And it's not just because of the joy of having a bed to myself. It's also because there's no more having to trail up to the spare room because of the insupportable snoring; no more having to crawl down to a cold sitting room in the middle of the night in case I wake a guy up by reading. No more moments when *he* wakes up in the middle of the night, turns on the light, and *doesn't* go up to the spare room, leaving me fuming with eyes sweating into an airline mask. No more bitter arguments when he insists on turning on Radio 4 at 7:00 a.m. and proceeds to sleep through it.

Evelyn Waugh said in his old age that he would rather visit the dentist for physical pleasure than share the marital bed—which was rather hard on Mrs. Waugh and, come to think of it, his dentist. And a third of women over sixty no longer sleep with their husbands—their men's snoring, fidgeting, and uncontrollable libidos force women into separate rooms.

Looked at from this angle, you know, the state of being single isn't so bad.

You're Not Alone in Feeling Lonely

Apparently 40 percent of Britons fear loneliness in their old age. The increasing desire of teen-agers to break away from the family and set up in a one-bedroom or even one-room apartment increases the feeling of isolation that plagues our society today. Fear, real or imagined, doesn't help—fear of walking the streets because you're certain you will be assaulted by muggers or rapists who won't stop, however friendly a smile you give them or however often you call them "darling" (see "Confidence"). Increasingly isolating laws, like those covering drunk driving, prohibiting smoking in public places, or requiring pubs and bars to have a license before they can even put on karaoke events, let along sing-alongs, force us out of a community and push us to indulge our addictions alone in our own homes.

More and more people yearn not for a partner to do things with but for a partner to do nothing with. More and more people are working from home, and some never meet their virtual work colleagues at all. I've never met my lawyer, even though she's drawn up my will, and have only met my accountant of five years once.

Don't be fooled into thinking that everyone else is out there having fun, relating to one another till they're blue in the face. They're not. There are loads of people just like you and me. Struggling. Getting on with it. Howling their eyes out in private, and in public insisting they're "fine." Remembering that can make you feel, oddly, less alone. More part of a loose-knit loneliness gang.

Lodgers

As I've said, I've always had lodgers. When I was broke I crammed so many of them into every nook and cranny that I often felt like an intruder in my own home; there is little more humiliating than returning from an evening out to find your kitchen stuffed with young people jabbering in Italian or Korean, staring at you rudely as if you were a gate-crasher.

The sharing-of-common-parts method is one way to have lodgers. But that has its drawbacks. What I hated about that particular lodger setup was that it made me so stingy. Every time I went to the loo I'd be counting the rolls of toilet paper. (Had she taken one to use as tissues?) Every time I went to the fridge I'd be counting the eggs. Or checking the garden to see if they'd left any cigarette butts in the borders. Or staring at the milk in the furious certainty that Someone Had Pinched a Bit.

And then I'd make secret forays into their rooms when they were away, sizzling with fury as I discovered my plates, broken, under the beds or, worse, the heater and the lights left on and the windows wide open.

But recently I've found a much more rewarding way of having lodgers. A loo and shower will fit into almost any tiny corner of the house and you can now buy mini freestanding kitchens that seem to be made for goblins, incorporating a tiny cooking range, wee fridge, minuscule sink, and a microwave the size of a small handbag. Thus I can have two lodgers sharing this lilliputian space who don't interfere with my living quarters in any way at all.

The house is now mine, all mine! The bathroom is mine and the fridge is mine. The freezer is clear of horrible bags of sweet corn and frozen factory-farm chicken breasts and boil-in-bag fish. I can play my music as loud as I like and leave the washing-up till morning.

And yet—and this is the joy of it—I'm not alone. I have my boarders upstairs. And on the odd night (say, once a week) when I'm assaulted by feelings of loneliness, I can simply wait, like a mugger, in my dressing gown in the dead-of-night darkness for one of the poor saps to stagger in—he's probably longing to go to bed—and chirp, "Good evening! And do you feel like having a quick nightcap?" And nine times out of ten the fellow is taken so unawares that he finds himself chatting in my kitchen till one in the morning just to assuage—most successfully—my lonely pangs.

Ballroom Dancing

My personal favorite. Even though I'm hopeless at it. It is not just a marvelously enjoyable way of exercising, but a brilliant way of being with someone else in an extremely intimate way without any sex, words, or whatnot. When I say "intimate" I'm not talking about the physical closeness. It's the way you have to mirror another's movements—just be with them psychically, to feel attuned and at one with another person. After an hour's worth of fox-trotting, I can only say I feel I'm floating on air.

Get in Touch with Yourself

Oh yes, it all sounds so easy-peasy: it's that insouciant "get in touch" as if it's as simple as writing a postcard, and of course it isn't easy at all. Some Indian sadhus have sat cross-legged at the top of mountains trying to get in touch with themselves for years. It's a hard slog.

The idea's seductive. Feeling lonely and isolated? Haven't got any friends? Hey—I've got an idea! Why don't you *make friends with yourself?* But when you try, you find that "yourself" isn't in, or has moved to Palo Alto or is sulking in her tent, or says she's got to wash her hair or that she'll call back and never does. (See also Talking to Yourself in "Ailments.")

It's still worth trying. Because there are two kinds of feeling alone. One is when we've just gotten divorced, or feel separated from everything and everyone—when we have simply lost connection with the world. We are not only without people to feel close to but, even when people are around, we still feel lonely. There is no lonelier spot than pressed by yourself against the wall at a party in full flow, surrounded by friends who are having a fabulous time.

But we don't necessarily need friends or lovers to keep loneliness at bay. There are other things we can connect with. We can connect with nature, rather like Henry Thoreau whose quotes kick off this chapter. He was a great promoter of the joys of solitude, and the presence of other people clearly made him feel rather sick.

If you can actually get a glimpse of those joys, of solitude rather than loneliness, it's pretty good. We have all had brief moments when, sitting in the garden with nothing but the birds for company on a sultry evening with the smell of woodsmoke in the air, we can experience real peace, a peace that can actually be ruined by someone else, even someone we love. We're in touch with nature, we feel that every robin is our friend, and every rose is speaking to us. I take the risk, I know, of sounding rather soppy and Madeline Bassettish. (Remember her? She was the ghastly P. G. Wodehouse character who believed that the "stars are God's daisy chain.") But sometimes we can feel part of a greater universe that some people call being in touch with God. Whatever it is, we can, briefly, feel part of a greater whole.

It's not that easy to feel like that when you're with someone else.

Pamper Yourself

I can't stand the words, of course—relic of my upbringing, I suppose. It was always thought it rather low-class to want to "pamper yourself," and certainly my elderly Scottish headmistress would have considered it tremendously self-indulgent when the alternative could have been reading an improving book about architecture. But if there's no one else to make you feel special, then, like the Little Red Hen in the children's book (and if you're under sixty you won't have heard of that either), you'll have to "do it yourself." Or, rather, pay for it yourself. A weekly massage needn't be that expensive, particularly if, instead of going to some high-falutin salon, you get it done by a brilliant Thai girl down the road. A nice bath oil can make your daily bath a pleasure—and for heaven's sake, if you just have a shower, do indulge yourself by getting the builders to squeeze a bath in, too, if you have room. Immersing yourself in hot water once a day is not an extravagant luxury. For lonely people, a long hot bath is almost (but not quite, of course) as good as sex.

Visit Old People

If you can't "get thee to a grannery," as one of my friends remarked when I told him I was far too busy with my grandchildren to see him—because if you don't have grandchildren to look after or they live too far away or you find the whole thing much too tiring—then visiting lonely old people can be a real treat. I'm not joking. I think everyone should have at least a couple of old people to go see. Not only are they usually extremely pleased to see anyone, they are fascinating company and often delight in making you a delicious snack as if you were a child on vacation. After you have visited them, too, you often feel not only young but noble as well, not feelings to be sniffed at.

Revel in Your Solitary State

Now you can have as many crumbs in the bed as you like. You no longer need to shave your legs. You don't have to apologize for being late coming home. You don't have to suffer the misery of finding that the person you're living with is suddenly, for reasons of his own, not speaking to you that day. You don't have to argue about who's in charge of the remote. You can also, as Katherine Whitehorn wrote in her autobiography, *Selective Memory*, delight in one of the very few pleasures she discovered after her husband died: "There is a sort of relief in not having to own up that you've been inept enough to drive from Kennington to Hampstead via a road labelled A23 Brighton."

Pets

If you have a garden, you could always try a cat. But get two. Cats like company just as much as everyone else and it's dotty to say they are loners. Also, get an old cat. If you're anywhere near sixty-five you don't really want the poor creatures to outlive you, which, were they to live for twenty years, they might well do. The animal shelter near me has a whole stack of ancient cats plaintively yowling as they wait to be rehoused.

Or you could get a couple of dogs. They get you walking and these creatures do at least get you up in the morning. There is a temptation, when you're single and old, to "go funny"—in other words, wake at 4:00 a.m., potter about, make a cup of tea, go on to Google, then crash out at 6:00 a.m. and not wake up till 10:00 a.m. If you need food that day, you might, as I have often done, put on a coat over your nightie, shove your feet into a pair of high-heeled shoes, and limp to the corner store for a few eggs and a paper. Stagger back, have a snooze after your scrambled-egg lunch, wake up to watch a bit of TV, and fall asleep over a book—without ever getting out of your dressing gown.

Disgusting, I know, but there it is. (When a friend calls during a day like this and asks me what I'm up to, I reply, sharply, "Working, of course! What do you think?")

So an animal of some kind is pretty crucial. It might at least prompt you to get dressed.

Old single ladies are traditionally associated with the keeping of cats, and I often have to stifle a yawn as my friends drone on about the antics of their own tedious furry friends. Sometimes you have to put up with a running commentary while you try to arrange a date on the telephone. "Thursday sounds fine," they say on the other end. "But Wednesday—oh, Oscar! You naughty boy! What are you doing that for?" Then, to me, with an indulgent chuckle, "That was just Oscar, jumping up onto my knee. Yes, Wednesday . . . I think he wants to talk to you! Oscar! Oh, your breath's a bit smelly, isn't it? You be a good boy and go and have some milk. . . . No, Oscar, not on my computer!" Then, to me, "You should see him! He's trying to get on my computer! He looks so funny!" Rest of the next five minutes spent with friend in uncontrollable giggles while I wait with pursed lips on the other end, still unsure when on earth we are meeting. And hoping that the ghastly Oscar won't turn up as well.

However, it was my friends' turn to yawn during the last year, as I became for a while completely infatuated with a pigeon. Call me sad, but we did have a real, genuine relationship.

It was no ordinary pigeon. It was a wonderful white creature with a bursting chest, a shimmering purple patch on its neck, a preposterous sprouting of a white crest on the back of its head, and an anonymous green tag on its leg. When he arrived he was clearly lost; he sat on my window day and night and pooped regularly on to my conservatory roof. Every so often I had to rush out to ward off neighboring cats. I fed him corn from my bathroom windowsill, and I seemed to be stuck with him. He loved human

217

contact and when I came into view, he turned one eye to me and shimmered at me through the window. Trawling the Internet I discovered that he was no ordinary pigeon. Oh no. He was a fancy pigeon, bred for display. And I didn't know anything about fancy pigeons.

I called endless fancy pigeon societies and asked if anyone might take him off my hands, but no one was interested. "But he's cold and lonely," I said, tearfully, to one pigeon-lover who answered the phone. "Lonely? Not likely!" he scoffed. "Why would 'e need a friend when 'e's already got one?"

"But he hasn't got a friend, that's the problem," I wailed.

"Oh yes, 'e 'as," the pigeon-man replied. "It's yew!"

The RSPB (Royal Society for the Protection of Birds) said that his breeder had probably deemed him a dud specimen and chucked him out of the aviary. My heart bled for him. I knew he was a wretched, lonely outcast. I was indeed his only friend. He, for a while, was mine, too. A terrible responsibility.

After consulting a biology professor friend, I hoped that come the spring his sex drive would force him into a relationship with another pigeon rather than an old lady, but after a winter of complete misery in which my pigeon spent his days and nights lonely and bedraggled and sitting alone on my neighbor's drainpipe, huddling into the wall with his beak turned into the corner when it rained, the spring arrived and the only other pigeons on the horizon were a greedy gang of ferocious, dusty, feral birds who arrived every morning to steal his food. He disappeared for a week once, but arrived back shivering, his feathers all awry, more gray with dust than white, and clearly traumatized. Now he never left his pipe except to make nervous forays for his corn. I became consumed by worry and compassion for this sad, abandoned bird.

Eventually the situation grew intolerable. Not only did my house become infested with cockroaches ("And that bird can't help," said the exterminator darkly, peering up through the pigeon's lavatory and giving it a dirty look as he put on his mask to spray the entire house), but I began to worry that by feeding him I was condemning him to a life of loneliness. His presence became a source of guilt and misery to me, too, as if I had my own personal Guantánamo Bay prisoner, wretched and alone, haunting me every day.

Everyone gave me different advice. "Stop feeding him!" was the most frequent. But how could I? He just hadn't been brought up to feed himself. And I knew I couldn't resist him if, thin and bedraggled, he came pecking at my windows on cold mornings.

I just had to find a home for him. And, luckily,

a friend said she knew of somebody who lived in a beautiful cottage in the middle of the Fens who absolutely adored birds. Not only did he have herds of guinea fowl racing across his lawn, he also had flocks of bantams. He also owned a dovecote (or *pigeonnier* if you want to be fancy) in the garden. If I could catch my pigeon, he would welcome him.

I devised a Heath Robinson kind of trap, which involved putting an old cat basket on the sill, with its door innocently open, and placing the pigeon's food and water inside. Eventually he started to venture quite deep inside—as did the other pigeons, of course—but on an appointed day I slammed the door shut on him, and, shaking with anxiety, dismantled the basket from the sill, locked it up, and covered it with a cloth.

My friend and I popped the bird into the trunk of her car, and drove for two and a half hours. I was sure he'd be dead of fright when we arrived, but he was still hanging on in there. When we reached our destination, the saintly bird-lover immediately took the pigeon up to his new home—a special kind of waiting room where he had to spend ten days before being released among the other birds, with his own covered balcony. After lunch, he emerged onto his balcony, looking as if he'd died and gone to heaven. I have never seen a bird look flabbergasted with delight before.

Not only that but other beautiful white male doves and fancy pigeons were flocking to see my bird, displaying all over the place. My mistake: it now became clear that "he" was a female bird.

Ten days later she was free, flying with the other birds, hopping along the lawn, preening herself on the trees in the autumn sunshine. Today, she is the mother of one. And, crazy as it is to get so attached to a pigeon, I miss her.

But, for a year, she certainly assuaged any feelings of loneliness.

Facebook

This is a tricky one because although various people have asked me to be their friend on Facebook, I've so far turned them down. So embarrassing. And it's almost as hard to refuse online as it is in real life. Up comes the e-mail: "Jonathan Bunter (or whoever) would like to add you as a friend on Facebook." And then you either have to ignore him, which seems incredibly mean and rude, or get in touch with Jonathan, whom you probably haven't seen for years, if ever, and explain very politely and friendlily, why you don't want to get involved, adding, of course, that it's nothing personal and ending with a sympathetic "Hope you're well" or some such. You then start an e-mail correspondence with him that can be almost as time-consuming as Facebook itself.

That's why I don't want to join Facebook. It would take up too much of my time. Time better spent missing my pigeon. "You won't have a moment to yourself," said a friend who'd gotten hooked. "Having joined Facebook, I now spend my entire life on the computer talking to friends, old school friends around the world . . . their friends . . . friends of their friends . . . it's completely addictive."

It's nice to know, however, that it's always there in case of a loneliness emergency.

Talk to People

Another friend of mine, widowed a few years ago, told me that although she has hundreds of friends and is out every night, she sometimes finds that she needs the sound of another human voice in the day, just to reassure her of who she is. I know the feeling. I've sometimes simply got dressed in order to go to the local library, discuss the weather with the librarian, exchange a book, and come home again, just to make clear the whole idea of who I am. It's all too easy, when being alone, to start to feel that you are just a nonperson, a glass of water poured into another glass of water. Without the boundaries that the presence of other people gives you, it's easy, in no more than a few hours, to imagine yourself as just a blob of nothingness. A small bit of conversation can usually put things right.

Recently I sat next to a man at supper who was, as so many people are doing these days, bemoaning the lack of community spirit in his street. "No one says hello anymore," he whined. "No one knows anyone."

"Do you say hello to your neighbors?" I asked.

"No, I don't know them," he replied, shaking his head gloomily.

"Well, why on earth don't *you* say hello first?" I asked, incredulously. "Why don't you start a residents' association? Ask them all to a party? Why don't you, instead of complaining, get out and do something for your community?"

"Um, yes, perhaps you're right," he said, rapidly changed the subject and started moaning about something else, while I turned to my other neighbor and hoped I'd find someone more interesting. (No such luck. He was a psychoanalyst.)

Get a Girlfriend

For those for whom an animal—be it a pony, a pigeon, or a cockroach—is not a suitable companion, here are two final thoughts. When I was young, lunch with a girlfriend or, worse, supper with a girlfriend was always a slight—very slight—sign of failure. There was always that feeling that appearing in a restaurant together meant you were two desperate females who couldn't get a guy. As we get older and the urgency to "get a guy" recedes, women friends are no longer second best. I'm not saying that a date with a man—any man (almost)—doesn't always hold a certain *frisson* for a woman. There is something about being with someone "other," be he three years old or ninety years old or gay as a Christmas tree, that still puts any woman on her mettle (and no doubt vice versa); in the presence of a man a woman will always feel more like a woman, and slightly sparklier.

But that's a different experience from being with a girlfriend. And, indeed, a good meet with a girlfriend can, if you have close enough contact (and I'm not talking here about physical contact or even confessional exchange, just the wonderful feeling of two people completely at ease with each other), be an experience that's almost as good as a brief moment during a love affair.

Because, as the lack of sexual interest makes men more accessible as real friends, so the same lack lessens the underlying tensions in female relationships. Other women are no longer a threat. And a lot of fun can be had looking back on the silly ways we behaved when we were younger, anxieties about being grandparents, not to mention a myriad ailments that you might not especially want to discuss with a fellow.

Get a Guy

It's true that "when an old man wants a young wife, it's for a nurse; when a young woman wants an old man, it's for a purse," but there's nothing wrong with that—it's a deal of a kind. But what about older women? Well, George Eliot first got married at sixty. And sixty-eight-year-old Barbara Windsor's latest husband is twenty-six years her junior.

Anyway, according to a survey by the American Life Project, the fastest-growing group of users of dating services and online daters is the sixty-five-to seventy-year-olds. So, if you really can't bear being on your own, try Internet dating. I have a single male friend whose romantic life consists of wining and dining different strange women he meets on the Internet. Some stick around for a couple of months. Some he sleeps with. Some he has one date with and then never again. But for him the steady flow of partners is almost like a permanent relationship, simply because there's no gap between women at all, as far as I can see.

I don't think that would suit me, but I do have two women friends who have met people on the Internet and have actually gotten married to the men they unearthed. Admittedly they changed their ages, losing about fifteen years apiece before, some months into the relationship, revealing the truth. And they did have to sift through hundreds of the creepiest, vilest, yukkiest frogs before they found their princes. But find them they did.

And if they can, you can.

16. Old Friends

Let us be grateful to people who make us happy, they are the charming gardeners who make our souls blossom.

—Marcel Proust

. . . . .

Senescence begins
And middle age ends
The day your descendants
Outnumber your friends.

—Ogden Nash

WHEN YOU'RE YOUNG it's impossible to have old friends. True, you can still keep up with someone from nursery school, but such a friendship can hardly be called "old." You need to have put in at least thirty-plus years of knowing each other before you can place each other into the "old friend" category, and by the time you're sixty, some of your friendships may well have lasted as long as fifty years. We have laid them down like bottles of wine in our youth, and now we can savor them—and often their flavor is good simply because they're old. Often, of course, it's not (they're corked, as it were), and we can curse ourselves with our lack of perception when we were younger as, year after year, we're obliged, simply out of good manners, to lunch with some turgid bore who, while no doubt huge fun to meet when we were making little figures out of plasticine when we were both three years old, has turned into a right-wing ranter at the age of sixty.

These old friends are extremely strange beings. Almost certainly, if you both bumped into each other for the first time in the present day, you wouldn't dream of becoming firm friends. You might find each other likable enough, but nothing to write home about. Yet an old friend who has shared so many experiences with you, often whose separate memories can almost duplicate your own, can be like wonderful old cardigans. They may have some holes in them, they may be cobbled up with bits of wool a slightly different color from the original, and the buttons—well, some are certainly missing and those that remain are sewn on with thread that doesn't match, and there may be a lack of stitching in the pockets, which means all your loose change slips through. But you can't bear to throw them away. They're just so comfortable. So old.

New Old Friends—Is This Possible?

A new old friend is something that sounds rather like a scientific impossibility, like perpetual motion. But the reason I always love meeting people whom I used to know slightly in my youth is that I think they can perhaps be transformed, against all the rules, into a brand-new old friend. God knows, we need them. As some poet said, "As life runs on, the road grows strange,/The milestones into headstones change,/Neath every one a friend." If we didn't constantly replenish the supplies, we'd soon be able to fit our entire address book on a postcard.

This is partly why reunions are such fun. You can't have a reunion when you're straight out of college (well, you can, but no one will have changed very much since you last saw them). But throw a reunion forty years later and talk about *coups de vieux*. (See "Looks.") Some people look so ancient as to be unrecognizable. Some people *are* unrecognizable. Thank God (we each think privately) that at least *we* have kept our looks up to a point. But then we find that within a couple of minutes the age in these old friends' faces just slips away. Suddenly we can barely remember them as they used to be—and yet they seem like the same old pals, all over again. And, as with finding all kinds of old trash in an attic, we root through these groups of old classmates in an effort to find, perhaps, someone valuable, someone special whom we'd completely ignored at the time or forgotten about; someone whom, maybe, we could dust off and who could then become transformed into another new old friend.

Bringing Old Friends Back to Life

Old friends, too, can be resuscitated, even if they've been chucked aside in your youth because of some falling-out. When you're old you can see things in much better perspective. Arguments with your ex, perhaps, which seemed insuperable at the time, now get less and less important the farther away you are from the incidents that prompted them. And another plus about getting old is the ability to forgive slights that have been harbored for years.

Even people you haven't spoken to for ages can be rehabilitated, simply because time has washed soft the hard edges that caused so much conflict in the first place. Age is a great forgiver. Suddenly it seems such a *waste* to chuck all that love and fun, which you must have experienced at some point for them and with them, down the drain. It's like throwing away a chicken carcass without making it into soup. Or digging and manuring an entire garden and then, just because of some stupid misunderstanding, refusing to plant anything in it. The passage of time means you can drag these old castoffs from the bottom of the psychic black sack to which they've been consigned, and realize that there was something worth preserving in there, after all.

They're important, these funny old things, often like gnarled, blackened old potatoes. Forget about them as people per se. One of the sad things about old friends and relations dying, apart from the obvious grief of losing them simply as people, is that you lose with them shared experiences, phrases, nicknames, jokes . . . that can never be revived with anyone else. So it's often worth hanging on, even to unsympathetic old friends, just for shared memories.

Warning

Do not under any circumstances introduce these old friends to anyone else. *You* may find them charming because of a buildup of memories and past kindnesses, but new friends will be horrified when you produce these smelly old Labradors, as it were, out of the woodwork. They would not dream of introducing *their* old friends to *you*—they are personal and private, and they'd no more want to share them than they'd want to share an old bath mat, particularly a bath mat covered with old black mold at the back (see Anxiety in "Ailments"). In case you think I'm being cruel, I'm completely aware that I am also other people's "old friend," and hope that they'll keep me in the background rather than introduce me to their newer models. When someone introduces me to a new friend of theirs as an "old friend," I cringe inside. I know that what they're saying is shorthand for, "Forgive my stupidity in accidentally getting you together. You won't understand her at all. She was someone I knew when I was young and silly, so please don't judge me on the basis of my knowing her. It's true that I love her, but it's just a foible." I imagine they feel like I might feel if someone submitted to the editor of the *Independent* a poem I'd written in elementary school.

With any luck, we've built up a bank of old friends to cushion us in our old age, rather like taking out a pension. It's true that some of these friends may, like pensions, have proven to be duds and barely deliver anything forty or so years on, but others prove surprisingly fruitful. And remember, as they say in the financial services, the value of your friendships can go down as well as up.

But on the whole, as a friendship consultant I'd always advise that unless they are toxic, it's worth hanging on to old friends, however dreary they may seem at the moment. You never know when the friendship market is going to change. It's always worth having a few cozy old friends in a dusty drawer for use in emergencies.

17. Time

. . . A letter from a lady who has described me in a French newspaper—"a noble lady with a shock of white hair"—Lord, are we as old as all that? I feel about six and a half.

> —Virginia Woolf,
> in a letter to Vanessa Bell

. . . . .

I will never be an old man. For me old age is always fifteen years older than I am.
—Francis Bacon,
sixteenth- and seventeenth-century philosopher

. . . . .

Seven ages: first puking and mewling,
Then very pissed off with your schooling,
Then fucks and then fights,
Then judging chaps' rights,
Then sitting in slippers, then drooling.

> —Robert Conquest

I'VE DISCOVERED SOMETHING rather odd about time. I was going away for a week to Scotland, and when I said to friends that I was dreading it—the older I get, the more stressful I find going away from home, notwithstanding that like a child at a party, I often "love it when I get there"—they said, "But it's only a week! Now that we're older it passes in a flash!"

In one way they're right because a week is only 1/3328 of my entire past life—rather short. But when I see it in terms of my future life (say ten years) it's 1/520—incredibly long.

When I think that I've already experienced sixty-four Christmases, it seems crazy to get into such a tizzy about it, and worry about where I will spend it or who will spend it with me. And yet when I think in terms of there perhaps being only ten more Christmases left, it doesn't seem as foolish to regard each Christmas as important.

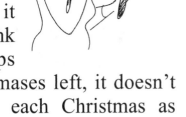

Regardless, before you know where you are, spring is here again, summer seems to be upon us, autumn is only a few days away, and Christmas does seem to come around with alarming frequency. As I'm still sweeping the old pine needles from the cracks between the cushions in the sofa, I can't think why I didn't just get a tree in a pot and keep it up, decorated, for the whole year. The prospect of clambering up a ladder and putting up those wretched old decorations yet again, only to pull them down two weeks later, seems dotty. Then there's the entire crib carved out of balsa by my father to assemble, not to mention the irritating little brass Austrian tinging thing with angels going round and round when you light the candles. Or not tinging. Or going around backward.

When I said to someone in 2010 that 2011 was around the corner, he replied, with an agonized sigh, "Oh dear, is there no end to it?" I knew exactly how he felt.

Time goes extremely fast when you're old. It's about the only thing that does, because in all other respects *you* yourself get slower and slower.

When Are We Officially Old?

"Oh, you're only as old as you feel!" trill some of my more ancient friends. But who do they think they're kidding? They must think like Jack Straw does, apparently, that they're "somewhere between eighty and thirty-five, depending what's happening that day. If you were born in the '60s you think you have a divine right to go on feeling young."

When we get old, all of us have that peculiar sensation of being at once quite childlike and at the same time utterly ancient. We're like one of those 3-D postcards you get in Greece, which, when you look at it from the left, shows an immaculate Parthenon decorated in gold and adorned with statues; when you look at it from the right, it's a crumbling old ruin. Other people's perceptions don't make anything any clearer either. In my experience, the young see you as old, but the old see you as a spring chicken. When I've told people of seventy the title of this book they've chuckled and then, putting a withered hand on mine, exclaimed, "But my dear, you don't even yet know the *meaning* of the word old!"

Every year that passes, time gets more confusing. Jean Rhys said that "Age seldom arrives smoothly or quickly. It's more often a succession of jerks." (As I well know; see "Sex.") And, I'd add, backward reverses as well. Anyway, isn't "old" not just how far you are from the beginning, but how close you are to the end?

My definition of getting old is when you can't do the seat belt up in other people's cars without fumbling and when you can't get out of them without using your hands on the side of the door to lever yourself upright. It's when you surreptitiously buy yourself a folding cane to keep in your bag "just in case" and when, if your papers haven't been delivered, you dare to shuffle down the street to the corner store in your slippers, with only a coat buttoned over your nightie.

In Germany you know you're officially old when you're offered a special menu. Apparently over there if you're young, you're offered a normal menu. If you have kids, you're offered a normal menu plus a kids' menu, a *Kinderteller*— beans and chips, probably—on the side. But if you're old, you're offered a *Seniorenteller*. You can imagine what that is. Very small portions. Mushy. And you're probably given a straw to suck it all up with. If you ask for a chewy steak or crunchy celery, you're no doubt told that "Sorry, you're too old."

Do You Tell?

When asked your age you can, of course, be enigmatic like Cary Grant. When someone sent his agent a telegram asking, "How old Cary Grant?" he sent back the reply, "Old Cary Grant fine. How you?"

Or you could just sigh and say, "Well, put it like this. I won't see sixty again."

But I don't like keeping my age secret. I always worry that someone knows how old I am and will then tell everyone behind my back. Much better that I should be the person to tell them first. My date of birth, just in case anyone wants to know, is February 3, 1944. No earlier and no later. It's all down there in Somerset House or wherever they keep birth certificates now (probably online, in a vast data center available to everyone in the world if they only knew the password).

What Do We Call Ourselves?

I like calling myself simply "old," but we can all facetiously describe ourselves as "oldies" or "wrinklies." When I phone to book tickets for a film or show, I sometimes ask, "Are there discounts for this?" And when the person at the other end says, "And what kind of discount are you?" I'm never sure whether to answer "Senior citizen" (or, as I once said, getting a bit confused, "Senior sitting room") or "Old-age retiree" or, as I usually do, in a quavering voice, "I'm just incredibly ancient, my dear."

I have considered calling myself a "New Age retiree," but then maybe they'd think I was one of those ancient long-haired, gray-haired people, wrinkly wrists covered with metal antirheumatism bands and grimy pieces of colored string.

We could call ourselves "elderly" or "senior," but I quite like "over the hill." Why? Because once you're over the hill you get a much better view of everything than when you are struggling up it. You can enjoy the grand panorama as you sail down. It's also an easier ride.

Seen It All Before

A friend once said that she got very depressed being alone day and night. Every day was the same, she moaned. But I pointed out that every day couldn't be the same because each new day she had more similar days behind her. It was this buildup of those same days that might, one day, push her into doing something to make tomorrow different. Time also gives us a completely different take on everything. It's difficult, quite honestly, to experience much as completely new because everything reminds us of something else.

I went to Venice recently. Extremely lovely. Very beautiful. But because I'd been before when I was young, what I was doing was retracing my steps from the last time I was there, remembering restaurants I'd visited and art galleries I'd seen. One of the things you *can't* do when you're old is see many things for the first time.

Time's Changes

Time changes people, too. It's in old age that leopards really *can* change their spots. I know several people who were lousy mothers who now make brilliant grandmothers. I know men who, once bright and clever and innovative, have turned into crabby old codgers who moan about "the youth today." I know an elderly woman who, during her later years, has softened completely and who is now a twinkly-eyed charmer whereas before she was terrifyingly critical and acerbic. And I know another woman who was stoned (no, not like in Pakistan; the other kind) most of her life, left each of her five husbands, had four kids by different men, but who now teaches yoga in a country village, is the pillar of her community, and is never absent from the church fete or the local charity run.

And isn't it great when time changes old boyfriends? From being golden gods at whose shrines you once worshipped, you meet them now and you can hardly hear what they say for the sound of the scales clattering to the floor as they fall from your eyes. I actually met an old boyfriend recently whose hair was two shades *darker* than when I'd known him in the '70s.

Then a couple of years ago I went to a party and saw a small, elderly figure with white hair, and I was stunned by a pang of recognition. For this was a man who, when I was in my twenties, I had simply doted on for about five years. When I say "doted," it's an understatement. "Idolized" would describe it better. I'd dreamed about him, I'd gotten pregnant by him, had an abortion . . . I'd even become a drug courier for him when he ran out of some unspeakable substance in his country cottage, and I thought he was absolutely the only man in the world for me. After a disastrous split, I'd never seen him again. Until now.

It took only a few minutes of listening to him burbling on about his belief in the power of Nordic gods, his new theory about Glastonbury, and the fact that he appeared to have done absolutely nothing except stay exactly in the same place since I last saw him, to realize that this was not just a man I no longer loved but a man whose company I should actually actively seek ways to avoid.

"I must go to the loo," I said, interrupting his flow, and I turned on my heels and left, breathing a sigh of relief. I was delighted to find that time had changed me and my feelings completely.

Time's New View

Time is a great educator. It teaches us to take the long view—one we could never have had when we were young and the past was only about six inches deep. These days we can cast our eyes over great mountain ranges of past, full of rivers and deserts, and get a much better idea of the whole. We slowly see life as a long continuum rather than a series of individual events strung together by periods of sleep.

The sweep of my past actually includes meeting my great-grandmother (I know I am at risk here of "Boring for Britain," but I'm old and I like it). She lived with a companion in a Gloucester Road hotel. She wore, I remember, a long skirt of black bombazine, a buttoned black top over a white high-necked blouse. On her head she wore a black hat with a veil, and in her hand she carried a silver-topped stick.

I've known times when no one had a car, no one had a television set, and the stores were closed on Sunday. E-mail, texting, and cell phones were unknown (see "Boring for Britain" again). The amount of change people of my generation have experienced in their lifetime is, I suspect, much more than anyone of thirty today will experience in their lifetime. It's astonishing that, in view of all this, we have managed to stay reasonably sane.

And as you age, you slowly start to realize that the world didn't begin with you and isn't going to end with you. You understand that you are part of an ongoing cycle —and this realization has a profound effect on how you live your life. When I got my first cat I never thought of it as my "first" cat. It was simply my cat. Now that I have had so many cats, I can understand that we come and go in just the same way as cats do—the only difference is that we usually live longer.

A friend of mine told me that when she became a grandmother and was photographed by her own children, she remembered that it seemed like only the other day that she, too, was photographed as a baby on her own grandmother's lap.

This relentless ongoingness came home to me sharply when recently I went to an Al-Anon meeting, the twelve-step group for friends, relatives, and children of alcoholics. I'd last been to this particular group about ten years ago, and, for about four years, had been heavily involved. In my time I'd been treasurer, secretary, publications officer, chair, and expected in some peculiar way to be welcomed back as some old, venerated Al-Anon sage. I climbed the same stairs. I smelled the same smell of cabbage. I entered the same room, with the same chairs. But there the similarity ended. The room was full of strangers! They greeted me warmly, as a complete newcomer, and it was hard to explain that I had been engaged as an integral part of that group in the past. And yet now I was completely forgotten. And all these people who were now carrying out the same positions, the same rituals—they, too, would one day be forgotten, just as I had been. Made me think.

As we realize we're part of this chain of humanity, we see that "the future" isn't just a matter of how many years we've got left, but that it is also our children's future, and our children's children's future. (Does this contradict my previous views on global warming and so on? Yes, it does. I contradict myself. Whatever. It's a perk of old age.) There was a moment when I thought that I'd just spend the rest of my money until I died (see SKIing, in "Spare Time") but now I keep working—no longer for myself, because I could live quite frugally, but for the prosperity of my son and his family when I die, and my grandchildren's grandchildren. When I'm asked how much I charge for a talk or a piece of writing, whereas a little while ago I'd simply be grateful to be asked to do anything at all at my great age, and hang the fee, I now think, No—that might help toward a down payment for a grandson's flat, or Maybe that would help a great-granddaughter through college.

There is a curious way in which us oldies can find pleasure in trying to beat time; already trying to contribute, and *matter* to someone, and make a difference, even after we're dead.

18. Never Again

One of the delights of being older is being able to control ideas. I have suffered all my life from a disease called Brains in the Head . . . in youth you keep bubbling with ideas. They may be foolish but you can't stop them. I've learnt not to suffer too much from the Brains . . . As you get older your judgement develops. One of my joys is having my mind stirred by a good book, and not feeling I have to go to the typewriter afterwards. There is nothing nicer than nodding off while reading. Going fast asleep then being woken up by the crash of the book on the floor, then saying to yourself, well it doesn't matter much. An admirable feeling.

—A. J. P. Taylor

IF THERE EVER comes a time when you're bemoaning your lack of youthful prowess, console yourself with the knowledge that listed below are the many things you will *never* have to do again in your *whole life:*

- Lose your virginity
- Go hitchhiking

- Have another period
- Sit on a committee
- Berate yourself for not having ever read Freud or Sartre
- Have a boss
- Go on your first date
- Fall in love for the first time
- Get pregnant
- Have to ask for a raise
- Have to please anyone else to keep your job
- Feel obliged to get drunk to keep up with the others
- Worry about being too hairy (or not being hairy enough)
- Wait to be picked for a sports team
- Wait for exam results
- Go on an interview
- Go to school
- Cook your first Christmas or Thanksgiving dinner
- Hear yourself saying that John Lennon really had something when he sang "All You Need Is Love"

- Dance the Twist
- Get your ears pierced
- Have an IUD put in
- Have an IUD taken out
- Be flashed by men in raincoats
- Learn how to ride a bicycle

- Do homework
- Learn how to swim
- Climb a tree
- Have an argument with your teenage children
- Get enraged by a daughter borrowing your clothes
- Be shocked or surprised by anything—you've seen it all
- Believe that a witch might be hiding under your bed
- Consider becoming a lap dancer
- Feel compelled, when faced with some kind of Italian campanile or clock tower, to walk up the five hundred steps of the stone spiral staircase to the top
- Try to make the Olympic swimming team
- Attempt to become prime minister
- Recite a poem in front of your parents' friends
- Submit a curriculum vitae
- Think Bob Dylan is a kind of god
- Discover that you can't clean brushes covered in high-gloss paint with water
- Make a fool of yourself by declaring that Disraeli and Lord Beaconsfield were two entirely different people
- *Mind* if you make a fool of yourself by declaring that Disraeli and Lord Beaconsfield were two entirely different people
- Sacrifice comfort for style

- Paint a ceiling
- Give two hoots for troubled pop stars in rehab
- Run up or down escalators
- Think about giving your seat up
- Rummage around in Topshop
- Go to an open-air rock festival or, come to think of it, an open-air *anything*
- Think twice before walking out of a film or play that fails to come up to scratch
- Defer to your elders
- Worry about what the world will be like in fifty years' time
- Do last-minute revision
- Attend a workshop
- Think about getting a tattoo
- Worry about the white-slave trade kidnapping you
- Go out on the prowl
- Be surprised by the evidence of corruption in politics
- Impress your friends at college by climbing up a tower in your town and hanging your underpants from the top

19. Wisdom

And now, every fresh day finds me more filled with wonder and better qualified to draw the last drop of delight from it. For up until now, I had never known time's inexpressible wealth; and my youth had never entirely yielded itself to happiness. Is it indeed this that they call growing old, this continual surge of memories that come breaking in on my inner silence, this contained and sober joy, this light-hearted music that bears me up, this spreading kind feeling and this gentleness?

> —Maurice Goudeket,
> *The Delights of Growing Old*

. . . . .

The afternoon of human life must also have a significance of its own and cannot be merely a pitiful appendage to life's morning.

> —Carl Jung

WISDOM IS RATHER a big word to apply to the kind of disorganized, random knowledge you acquire as a result of having lived a long time. I think I'd prefer to describe this condition as "not being quite such a total fool as one used to be"—rather a different kettle of fish than "wisdom." But although we're always prone to making new mistakes, there's no question we don't make quite as many of the old ones. In other words, experience pays off. If there's not a pot of gold at the end of the rainbow, then at least there isn't exactly a pile of old rubble.

Here are a few scraps I've gleaned over the years.

1. There are two sides to every question. No, that doesn't mean that one can never be right. I'm *always* right, no doubt about that. But as I age, I do concede that other people may have other views. Wrong views, maybe. Mad views. Misguided views. But views.

2. We know we can't believe everything we read in the papers. Indeed, we know that we can hardly believe anything we read in the papers at all.

3. We know that while it's quite acceptable to write a letter to someone we feel furious

with in the heat of the moment, it's a great mistake to mail it. We have learned this from hideous experience, and still wake in the night when we think about that horrible note we sent to a friend way back in 1955 who later married that dreadful man who died in a skiing accident, and we're still sure somehow it was all our fault.

4. But then again, was it really our fault? Nah. We don't feel quite so guilty about things as we used to because we know that actually, our contribution to the world's good or ill is so minuscule as to be barely noticed, we are but ants . . . and so on.

5. We're not quite so dominated by our emotions as we used to be, and we know that whatever happens, it doesn't matter a helluva lot. We know that "these things, too, will pass" and that applies to the good times as well as the bad times.

6. We find it hard to worry about global warming or the end of civilization as we know it because we know that whatever happens will happen, *que será, será*, and because we suspect that in the end, it will all come out in the wash. This is a great relief. (If you don't agree with me on this one, see 1. I'm right—but I am also aware you have a view on this if it makes you feel any better.)

7. The less future we have in front of us, the more we can enjoy the now, and we have no regrets. We're happier with our lot, because we know that man is born to sorrow as the sparks fly upward and instead of cherishing unrealistic expectations of future happiness, we have caught on that if things aren't too bad right now then that's about as good as it can get.

8. When someone makes an unpleasant remark about us, either directly or behind our backs, rather than shrink into abject hurt and humiliation, it does occur to us that "Maybe they're jealous."

9. We often can predict the endings of films even before the initial credits have finished rolling, and we know, in a whodunit, that there's always the chance that the detective himself will have dunit.

10. We've seen changes in fashions, we've seen skirts go up and down, and we know that what goes around comes around. Which may make us seem a little jaded, but at least we know there's nothing new under the sun.

11. Somerset Maugham said that old people tend to be kinder and more compassionate than they were as young people—less sexual, less competitive, and less envious. It's true. Where the idea of people becoming crabbed and bitter in their old age came from, I don't

know. (Though perhaps it was because of people like Rev. Henry Worsley [see "Boring for Britain"].) Old people's minds function in a different way from young people's. The older you are, the sunnier your outlook on life. Apparently retirees view the world through rose-tinted glasses, filtering out bad memories in favor of more pleasant ones. When researchers asked two groups of adults—one in their twenties and the other in their seventies—to look at photos both of disturbing and untroubling scenes, and then asked them a half-hour later what they recalled, the older group struggled to remember nasty images; analysis of their brain scans revealed differences in the way they had stored the details of the pictures. The elderly had a much stronger link between the emotional part of the brain and the frontal cortex, which does more abstract thinking, allowing them to dilute any unpleasantness. In other words, we're *nicer*.

12. We know exactly the difference between being in love and loving and we know that we much prefer the latter. We also know that when a partner says he "wants more space" it's a euphemism for saying the relationship, in his view, is as dead as a doornail.

13. If we lend someone money, we no longer have any expectation of seeing it ever again.

14. We now realize, with some irritation, that when we were young and insecure everyone else was, too, even though they all seemed tremendously suave and adept at the time. Sometimes it crosses our minds that quite a few of us still feel exactly the same, even now. To our astonishment we realize that some people are actually terrified of us still—yes, funny, little, mild, insecure, hopeless, lowly-wormy old us. Very strange.

15. One friend said that it was such a relief, as one got older, to feel that the "cameras are off me," and I know what she means. We're not quite so concerned about what other people might say if we said or did something. We are able to be more ourselves. We are more comfortable in our own skins.

16. We know that life is too short for an argument. And we are more forgiving, not just of other people's behavior but also, thank God, our own.

20. Grandchildren

But the nicest thing about this second childhood is the link it brings with the first childhood! When a year ago Phyllis and I were sitting with a circle of grown-ups in the Doctor's Waiting Room waiting our turn to be called into the surgery, there was a tiny toddler, too little for me to know whether it was a baby-boy or a baby-girl. But after a few minutes of surveying each other, this tiny tot waved its hand to me, and I waved back! It was just as if we had said to each other: "Lord! What fools these grown-ups be!"

—John Cooper Powys,
in a letter to Nicholas Ross

WHEN I WAS YOUNG and gloomy, everyone would say, "Don't worry—soon Mr. Right will come along on a white horse and carry you off and everything will be all right!" They didn't say, as they should have done, "Don't worry! If you play your cards right, your heart may be captured by a small red sausage with a wrinkly face, wearing diapers, a tiny fellow who will one day call you 'Granny!' " The Welsh say that

"Perfect love does not come along until the first grandchild," and they're right.

What was so peculiar was that no one had alerted me to this possibility. It was as if I'd gone to the guidance counselor at school and she'd given me millions of options, but failed to mention that at some point in my life—if I played my cards right—I could become a grandmother.

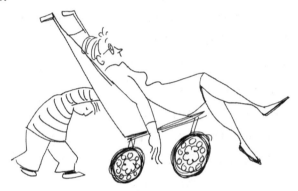

My grandchildless friends think my devotion to being a granny is idiotic. They tell me to "get a life," as if I haven't already got one. They tell me I'm crazy every time I put off going to see some ghastly play at the National Theatre in order to babysit my grandsons. "They're asleep, for Chrissake!" they say. "They could get anyone to watch them! Why you?" But I would rather sit downstairs in a quiet house listening to my grandsons' regular baby breathing on the monitor for hours on end than see some self-serving actor enunciating his socks off as Hamlet. I'd rather know that if my grandsons wake, someone who loves them will be there instead of a responsible stranger. Just pottering about aware that they're upstairs sleeping, small fingers stuffed into mouths, gives me a glow that pervades until the next day.

They do say that grandchildren are the reward you get for not killing your children. And Margaret Mead, the great anthropologist, memorably observed that the reason grandparents and grandchildren get along so well is because they "share a common enemy."

For a while, like all mothers of only children— and a son, at that—I'd sensibly put the idea of grandmotherhood out of my mind. I believed that the chance of my son's ever having children while I was alive was such a remote possibility, I couldn't even contemplate it—even though he was just thirty-two when I turned sixty. I tried to avoid possible disappointment by imagining that if he did get together with someone, it would be with an Australian and they'd emigrate and never be seen again. Best not to hope at all, I decided. There are thousands of us, trying to whistle a happy tune in order to prevent ourselves from blurting out, to our childless children, "But when are you going to settle down? And when are you going to *give me* grandchildren?"

It's that "give me" that they can't tolerate. And understandably. The idea of a granny standing by with a huge butterfly net waiting for the grandchild to pop out and then carrying it off as a trophy must be a horrifying prospect for any self-respecting couple.

But if a grandparent plays her cards right, she can become a support rather than a threat. Sixty-five percent of grannies take an active part in caring for grandchildren. And the joy of actually being needed by anyone when you're old is a real treat. To be needed because you can look after the delightful creatures who are your grandchildren is a double treat. The other plus to being a granny is that research has shown that families with strong grandparental connections are likely to have more stable children. Grandparents are close to the child, but also sufficiently old to be wise, and sufficiently removed from a family to be able to offer advice on how to deal with problems they may have with their parents. I often think of grandparents rather like the European Court of Human Rights. The Italians have a saying that goes, "If nothing is going well, call your grandmother," and it's true —if your mum has punished you and your dad has disapproved, a grandparent can perhaps shed new light on the whole incident and throw understanding on a situation to relieve the black-and-whiteness of the issue.

Of course, everything about grandchildren is completely different from How It Was in Our Day. Before the baby arrives, there are the sonograms—unknown at the time to our generation. And always incredibly difficult to decipher. A sonogram is rather like those photographs you sometimes see featured in a newspaper of a cloud, say, in which the Virgin Mary is visible to those who can make her out. And didn't someone once see Christ in a piece of toast?

No doubt due to my failing eyesight I could never decipher the image I was supposed to see in the sonogram photograph of my first grandchild—and felt rather like I did when, as a child, I was presented with a puzzle picture of a forest and had to find how many goblins there were hiding in the gnarled branches. So when my son showed me the scan of my first grandson, I, like many a granny before and after me, was forced to bluff. "Oh, yes I can see . . . yes, his tiny face . . . his little smile. . . ." My son looked at me witheringly. "Mum! He's only just developed legs. He hasn't got an *expression!*"

Strangely, when I was a young mum more than thirty-five years ago, I wasn't nearly so taken with life with a toddler. I remember sitting in gloomy playgrounds staring at my watch and thinking that I would rather be dead than spend another minute there. I remember the sheer grinding misery of getting up morning after morning at the crack of dawn to give the screaming child his breakfast, not to mention the endless, deadly days of freezing parks, broken sleep, and minced-up meals, the hopelessness that dogged me every day, every week, every month. And when my son cried, I'd be tortured by feelings of being a bad mother who never should have brought him into this cruel world.

What is so immensely rewarding and fulfilling about being with my grandsons is that my love for them is pure and clear, unclouded by all the guilt, panic, and anxiety I felt with my own son when he was tiny. I don't have that sense of "Oh, Lord, he's tired and listless, he must hate me." Or, "Oh dear, if I do this or don't do that, it will ruin him for life." If by chance one of my grandsons suddenly starts crying or yelling his head off, I'm guilt-free. Experience tells me that his fears are only tiny clouds in a fundamentally blue sky, and they will, with enough kisses and cuddles, pass.

Now I find myself, with my grandchildren, with all the time in the world. I'm happy to walk at the pace of a snail if that's what's required. And when we go to feed the ducks, I specially grind up some bread in the thingy, then put the crumbs into a plastic bag and off we go and I watch the youngest giving out the bread. First he puts his hand inside the bag, then he clasps the crumbs, not letting any spill. Then he withdraws his hand and turns in the direction of the ducks and—this is the clever bit—he releases his fingers as he throws the crumbs *in their direction*. He can feel, he can grasp, he can hold, he can gauge the right direction, he can release his fingers, and he can throw. I mean it's just brilliant, don't you think? I look at him. He's so clever. And he's so *kind*—he wants to feed the dear little ducks. He's clever and kind! What more could you want?

A grandmother used to be a woman with no teeth, a bun on her head, someone surrounded by a perpetual smell of a mixture of peppermints and cabbage. And, perhaps, rather stale pee. Grandfathers were bent figures with whiskery beards and pipes, always eager to teach anyone passing the rules of chess. But we baby-boomer grannies are a different lot. We think we have as much energy as we used to when we were young (but golly, how wrong we find we are, after a day with a couple of exuberant kids) and we want to be hands-on.

Of course, there are problems. For instance, what are we called, in this day and age? I have friends who, fearful of the label "Granny" giving away their age, shout, "Don't call me Granny!" and insist on being called by their Christian names. Another demands to be called Glammy— but not for me such euphemisms. I'm a granny, and I want to shout it from the rooftops. I'll even put up with the unsettlingly prophetic Gaga, which my first grandson called me for a while.

Another problem comes for our own children.

My son was amazed to find that not only had he become a father, but that his mother, in the space of about five minutes, had turned into a granny. When I arrived at the house crying, "And how are you, my lambiest lamb?" he'd be telling me how exhausted he felt from being up all night with my grandson, when he discovered that I had zoomed past him to speak to the baby. "Oh, did he have a sleepless night then, my little pet? Did we have a tummyache? Were we teething? My poor little darling!"

"A mother becomes a true grandmother," said some wit, "the day she stops noticing the terrible things her children do because she is so enchanted with the wonderful things her grandchildren do."

Certainly I can't help feeling rather delighted when I hear the grinding of my own son's teeth as he kindly asks my grandson the same question as I used to ask him, when they walk back from school: "And what did you do at school today?"

Back comes the inevitable reply: "Nuffink!"

The other problem is that we may think we're up-to-date, but we're not. We have to compete with child-care gurus such as Gina Ford who, as far as I can gather, believes every child should be left to scream for hours before it's picked up. We have to grit our teeth as young moms insist that children with temperatures should be left in cold rooms rather than, as happened in our day, put to bed swaddled with blankets and a hot-water bottle, to "sweat it out." We have to keep up with the latest fads on whether a child should be put to sleep on its tummy, its side, or its back. We have to be very careful not to air our subversive liberal views on thumb-sucking, pacifiers, or "time-outs."

Ah well, no doubt it'll turn out okay in the end. They buck you up, your mum and dad. . . .

Naturally we had to put up with our own mothers and mothers-in-law insisting on ideas promoted by some tyrant named Dr. Truby King, who recommended that children who masturbated should wear splints on their hands to prevent the dreadful activity. And *our* children, poor things, have to put up with us '60s grannies who believe that anything goes. We feel that we turn, once we become a granny, from being a mother to some wise and prehistoric person, but it's an illusion. To our children, frankly, we're just out-of-date.

And we have to not only go along with the new baby credo, but also untangle the new baby gadgetry.

One granny I know has the folding cot (that she bought when her baby granddaughter came to stay) still up in the spare room six years later. The reason? She is simply unable to dismantle it. The instructions have long been lost, and although every so often she goes up to wrestle with it, and has at least been able to fold up three of the sides, the fourth remains obstinately rigid.

When I was a young mum I had a traveling cot that consisted of four poles and a sling of canvas in between; the stroller was a light iron structure plucked from a construction site; the carriage, a portable baby bed on wheels. Today health and safety regulations mean that not only do you need the brain of a first-class engineer to get the grandchildren's accessories working, but to manage first to unfold, then manipulate, and then refold whatever gadget you've got requires the mental capacity of a Rubik's Cube champion.

One friend of mine had to put an open stroller into her trunk because she was unable to fold it up; another couldn't unfold the stroller and as a result had to carry both the baby and the folded stroller miles down a country lane. Yet another was unable to undo the brake and had to wheel her granddaughter all around the park at an angle on two wheels so, instead of the ducks, the child was only able to see the sky.

Even if you do understand how the wretched things work, your hands just aren't as strong as they used to be. When he was about eighteen months old, I was unable to fasten the catch on my grandson's car seat, and had to improvise by tying a plastic bag to one side of the seat, and then tying that to the finger of a glove, and knotting the whole thing up with a rubbery thing with hooks on the end that you use for keeping suitcases and furniture on the top of your car. In the end, the poor child looked like one of those strange and sinister parcels you sometimes see on the luggage carousel at the airport, a parcel that has apparently been there for years and looks like it will be there for a few years to come. I drove back very slowly indeed, one hand on the wheel and the other on his tummy in case he should suddenly propel himself out through the windshield.

Another time I couldn't get his straps open at the other end of the journey. After ten minutes he was yelling and I was crying and feeling so desperate that I was forced to enlist the help of a passing hoodlum who naturally managed to free him at once.

(There are, if you search the web, granny-friendly products available. There's a special hip sling for you to wear that enables you to carry a baby without doing your back in, simple travel cots, comprehensible strollers, booster seats, sing-along CDs for those ghastly car journeys that feature traditional counting songs, a bath-kneeler, potties, and even a safety pack so you've got everything by you in case of emergency.)

Grannydom flung me into the world of knitting. It threw me back into toy stores where I could browse for hours and find, to my astonishment, that books like *The Very Hungry Caterpillar*, *The Cat in the Hat*, and *The Tiger Who Came to Tea* were still going strong, which was rather a relief. I now search out information on the Net about how to rear tadpoles. I collect bits of candy wrappers, feathers, and colored straws so that we have enough material for collage and painting sessions when my grandsons come to visit. I can't see a picture of a cow without saying "Mooooo" or a dog without saying "Woof-woof!" It's got me digging out old recipes for gingerbread men, cheese straws, peppermint creams, and scones. The whole house often smells of baking these days as, after a series of disappointing disasters that had everyone in tears, I practice my skills. ("But Granny, what's happened to their *eyes!*" sobbed my grandson when all the gingerbread men came out looking like obese day-trippers, blinded by the sun.)

I feel an unaccustomed joy with my grandchildren, a joy that I've not had in any other relationship—and I'm not the only one. No cowboy was ever faster on the draw than a grandparent pulling a baby picture out of a wallet. And fellow grannies agree that the experience is astonishing, as marvelous as finding, in winter, a solitary rose blooming on a withered branch. (Actually it's a lot better than that, but you get the gist.) I read recently a quote from G. K. Chesterton, who wrote a hundred years ago that family is "this frail cord, flung from the forgotten hills of yesterday to the invisible mountains of tomorrow"—and when you're a grandparent it all becomes clear. The realization that life is just a string of people, generation after generation, going on forever, suddenly comes home to you in a way it never could without a grandchild.

Small wonder that these days I start calling my grandsons by my son's name, my son by his father's name, and his father by my grandson's name. We all seem to be floundering around in one big familial soup.

Sometimes I wonder if the seeds of my fulfillment in the role of granny hadn't been sown years and years before, with my own grandmother. She was my lifesaver. She lived below us in our house in London, and when things got too tense within my parents' loveless marriage, I would go downstairs and find her in her cozy living room, eyes twinkling, full of jokes and affection. She had a magical cupboard stuffed with toys and board games like Chutes and Ladders and Ludo. During hot summers we'd sometimes take a picnic out to the park and eat sugar sandwiches as a treat. She had always wanted to be a comic actress—she constantly sang me the old songs and even took me to see Joyce Grenfell, Flanders and Swan, and even the Crazy Gang. And since I was a lonely only child, I looked forward each year to the time when I would spend a week with her at the seashore, just the two of us. We'd take bags of plums down to the beach each day and, in the evening, visit the carnival down the road. I still remember the sound of the waves mixed with the music from the merry-go-round and the screams from the Big Dipper. Whatever ride I went on, my grandmother was always waiting for me at the end, eyes bright with excitement: "Was it *very* scary, darling? Was it fun? You're such a *brave* girl!"

When I painted a picture my parents would say, "Oh, fine. Now, have you done your homework?" But if I showed it to my granny, she'd open her eyes wide with astonishment. "Did you really do this? No, you're joking! It's just not possible. Let me look at it in the light! But darling, it's quite astonishingly good! It's quite wonderful! Would you mind if I got it framed and hung it up in my sitting room so everyone can see it? You draw quite superbly . . . and those colors! Darling, you're quite *amazing!*"

Grandparents share a curious granny camaraderie. The other day one told me about her two granddaughters, one being three years old and the other only nine months. They each had a teddy and she was planning to knit a sweater for both bears.

The older granddaughter declared that she wanted hers to be sparkly, with gold and pink and silver threaded through, and a star motif on the front. Asked what kind of sweater her granny should knit for her young sister, who was too young to speak her wishes, the child replied, with an evil glint in her eye, "I think gray would be *very* nice."

My own grandson once crept into my bed at five in the morning, claiming that he had woken early because he had had a "deem about piders."

"Granny? Granny?" he'd said, when he'd finally managed to wake me up. "I got good idea. You go down the end of the garden and be *monster,* and I get my *sword* and I be *knight* and come and *kill* you!"

And a little while later as I stood, waiting behind a tree shivering in my glamorous dressing gown in the cool dawn light at the start of a long, long day, while my grandson charged toward me with his plastic sword, I realized I was happy.

Isn't it great, being old?

permissions

"What Fifty Said" from *The Poetry of Robert Frost* edited by Edward Connery Lathem, published by Jonathan Cape. Reprinted by permission of The Random House Group Ltd.

Virginia Woolf letter from *The Letters of Virginia Woolf* by Virginia Woolf, published by Hogarth Press. Used by permission of the executors of the Virginia Woolf Estate and The Random House Group Ltd.

Diana Athill quote from Diana Athill interview with Kira Cochrane. Copyright Guardian News & Media Ltd 2009.

Maurice Goudeket, *The Delights of Growing Old*, reproduced by permission of Pollinger Ltd and Maurice Goudeket.

John Cooper Powys quote reproduced by permission of Pollinger Ltd and the Estate of John Cooper Powys.

"Ain't It Grand to be Bloomin' Well Dead." Words and music by Leslie Sarony ©

Center Point Publishing
600 Brooks Road ● PO Box 1
Thorndike ME 04986-0001 USA

(207) 568-3717

US & Canada:
1 800 929-9108
www.centerpointlargeprint.com